WILEY HALL

Kenneth A. Pettit

Order this book online at www.trafford.com
or email orders@trafford.com

Most Trafford titles are also available at major online book retailers.

Printed in the United States of America.

ISBN: 978-1-4907-1100-3 (sc)
ISBN: 978-1-4907-1102-7 (hc)
ISBN: 978-1-4907-1101-0 (e)

Library of Congress Control Number: 2013915431

Trafford rev. 08/26/2013

 www.trafford.com

North America & international
toll-free: 1 888 232 4444 (USA & Canada)
fax: 812 355 4082

Contents

Acknowledgments

The following people and publications are acknowledged as being important to the creation of this book. Their encouragement and support lifted my spirits, jogged my memory, and made me face my past. The experience was chicken soup for my soul. I shall be forever grateful for them.

Virgilius "Leo" Dibiase, a Home Kid

George "Sellars" Sellars, a Home Kid

John "Johnny Vee" Vafiades, a Home Kid

Thomas R. Yacovella, a Home Kid

Frank, a Home Kid

All the Home girls, not mentioned very much

All Home Kids, past and present

My Canadian cousin, Wayne Pettit, not a Home Kid

The old folks, the jewels of the Home

Freemasons, State of New York

Masonic Care Community

Frank's speech, Reunion 1988 *Appendix A

Newsweek, December 12, 1994

One Hundred Years of Service to Humanity, Masonic Home Centennial, October 16, 1993

"Outline History of Utica and Vicinity," prepared by New Century Club, LC Childs & Son, 1900

Utica Observer-Dispatch, September 1, 2012

Wall Street Journal, November 29, 1994

Introduction

In 1842 a dollar was placed upon an altar. Thereafter, ten pennies were assessed to each New York State Mason. That dollar and those pennies created "an Asylum for worthy and destitute Masons, their widows and orphans." It was believed in the nineteenth century that government did not care for orphans and the needy. There is no more lonesome word in the English language than *orphanage*. In 1851, 150 acres were purchased in Utica, New York, for "the Asylum for the Aged, Infirm Brothers, the Destitute Widows and the Helpless Orphan." The Masonic Home and Asylum (now the Masonic Care Community) opened its doors to the orphans and the needy in 1893 having been dedicated on October 5, 1892. The price for the land was $10,000 and for buildings and equipment, an additional sum of $10,000.

Construction on the site began prior to the arrival of the orphans and elderly. The administration building was erected and dedicated in 1891-92, followed by the Knights Templar Building, Soldiers and Sailors Memorial Hospital, the Charles Smith Infirmary, the nursery (now the Livingston Library), the Daniel D. Tompkins Memorial Chapel, the Wiley Hall, and the

Vrooman Building. Each cornerstone was solemnly laid in the southwest corner true to the Square and level with the Plumb in accordance with the Great Architect of the Universe. These gothic structures stood for years.

No home is complete until its gardens, lawns, and trees are planted. This task fell upon the sturdy shoulders and strong arms of several Italian immigrants, fondly referred by the kids as the Tonys. These men braved the hot, muggy summers and ice-cold winters in order to make a haven for the residents. Their pay was a pittance.

A vital piece of the Home was placed when the trustees of the New York State Grand Lodge appointed William Wiley as superintendent. For the next forty years, "Pop" Wiley and Mrs. Wiley were the people in charge; the mainstays, if you were. They were the first and last word. Discipline, decorum, and parceled-out love were evident for the next four decades and, to a certain extent, beyond. The administration was vertical, top-down. At times, it appeared that the skills of those in charge were the ability to see lightning and hear thunder.

A cult of the individual was ingrained with the following "Happy Birthday with Our Love" poem from the nursery kids.

Hickery, dickory dock, the mouse ran up the clock,
The clock struck Nineteen Forty-five
And the prayers said in 1910 are still alive.
God Bless Mama Wiley, God Bless Papa Wiley.

They tried to make it a "home."

In 1923 a slice of heaven was created with the purchase of 1,600 acres in the Adirondack Mountains. The camp served as the outlet for the kids' pent-up hibernation of the autumn, fall, and spring months spent in Utica. For two months, the kids could explore the forest, climb the mountains, and fish the lake, ponds, and streams. Ghost stories abounded, sports were engaged in, shooting stars and fireflies sparkled the moonless nights. No one liked going back to Utica.

The Home became populated in May 1893 with children and elderly folks. In 1899, 190 adults and forty-eight children took refuge. It has been chronicled that a total of 969 children entered the Home. The stories that follow tell the stories of those Masonic Home citizens.

Read, remember, enjoy.

Prologue

We were different. We dressed alike. We had a mother or a father or none. We covered the face of Europe, Canada, and America. We were all brothers and sisters. Our blood was different, but we were all brothers and sisters. One died in infancy; others lived four score and more. Some died in battle. Some died in peace. And some died in torment.

We were welders, engineers, scientists, doctors, and nurses. We were lawyers, judges, and elected officeholders and bankers. We were cabdrivers, artists, musicians, and teachers. We were military officers, enlisted soldiers, sailors, and marines. One guarded the Tomb of the Unknowns. One was a priest. We were farmers and pharmacists. We were athletes and scholars. We were husbands, wives, aunts, uncles, and grandparents. We created successful children. We were religious and rebellious, faithful and sinful. We all laughed and we all cried. We were different.

We slowly began to disappear. The advent of social welfare programs, social security, and the increased costs of institutional support all lent themselves to the disintegration of the orphanage. The conscious decision to turn the Masonic Home into a Masonic Care Community was the death knell. No more Home Kids. The inconspicuous plaque in front of the Tompkins Memorial Chapel is the sole reminder that 969 children entered the Home. We became but a footnote in Masonic history. We will not be denied our history.

We will not disappear. Listen to the winds and place your ear against the ground. You will hear the collective voices of 969 Home Kids.

Epilogue

The writing of these short stories was both a challenge and a joy. My memory was tested in order to recall names and happenings. The experiences were sometimes hurtful but the people were the salve. All in all it was a healing process. What were the fates of these people?

Virgilius Dibiase, after being kicked out of the Home served a tour in the United States Air Force and graduated from Northeastern University. He became an electrical engineer and started his own company. He married and has two children- a physician and a lawyer. He is retired and resides in Belmont, Massachusetts.

Thomas Yacovella graduated with honors from Syracuse University. He served in the United States Army and became a well-recognized wildlife artist and author. He is married with two fantastic children - a physician and a daughter who allows me to call her Steeeeve. Tom currently resides in Utica, New York.

Bernard Yacovella, like his brother, graduated from Syracuse University. He became an engineer, married and has three outstanding daughters. He is retired and currently resides in Vero Beach, Florida.

George Vafiades graduated from the University of Buffalo, served in the United States Army and became a licensed pharmacist. He is married, has three successful sons and currently resides in Lake Katrine, New York.

John Vafiades graduated with honors from the University of Rochester. He joined the United State Air Force and served with distinction as a Captain. A lifelong bachelor, John reads and grows vegetables on a mountain top in Westfield, Pennsylvania.

George Sellars, a college graduate, served in the United States Navy. He is a metallurgist, married with five children, is retired and currently resides in New Hartford, New York.

James Sellars, an All-American football player from the New York State University at Cortland, joined the United States Navy and held the rank of Lieutenant Commander. He is married with two sons and currently resides in Torrance, California.

George Karros graduated from Yale University and served as a Captain in the United States Marine Corps. He is married and has two sons—a major league baseball player and a certified public accountant. George currently resides in San Diego, California.

Richard Larsen, upon graduation from high school, left the Home and joined the United States Navy. He lived his dream and sailed the world. His ship ported in Staten Island, New York, He is married, became a banker and is a lay minister.

Kenneth Pettit graduated from California State University, Long Beach. He was elected to public office and served four terms. He has three children and currently resides in Santa Barbara, California.

Brad O'Hara bravely and successfully challenged the world. He currently resides with his twin brother in the State of Washington.

Rudy Valenzl graduated from Utica College, was drafted into the United States Army and was appointed as camp counselor. He became a director of the YMCA, New England region. Sadly, he committed suicide.

Fred and Marilyn Dunlap graduated from universities. Marilyn became a teacher as did Fred who was drafted into the United States Army. Each served together has camp counselors. Fred was honored with an endowed chair at his alma mater, Colgate University.

Frank and Mary Ellen Hall served the Home as the boys' patron and matron, respectively, They passed away in the 1970's. They were smokers.

William T. Clark, M.D. and Violet Clark served the Home for more than thirty years, Doctor Clark ushered in a much needed reformation. They passed away and headstones were dedicated in their memories on Pine Point at Round Lake, Woodgate. New York.

July 18, 1944

~

Everyone has a birth date, a commencement of life, or
a specific time when knowledge, feelings, and growth
appear and mature. My physical nascence was March 13, 1940.
On that Wednesday morning, I was ushered into the world
not through the warm and fluid uterine canal but lifted from
my mother's womb with the sharp edge of a physician's scalpel.
Later in life I would discover that I was a cesarean section baby.
My mother, a thirty-year-old housewife and mother of three
boys, simply did not have the physical ability to deliver me
through the normal birthing process. She was in the advanced
stages of ovarian cancer. Twenty months later, she died at age
thirty-one.

For the next three and a half years, my father took on the
chore of raising four boys. My two oldest brothers, Chuck
and Bob, often performed roles of surrogate parents for me
and my brother Jim. My father emigrated from Thunder Bay,
Ontario, Canada. He left the poverty of the farm in this native
western Ontario province during the '20s. Farming was not in
his dreams. He tried bootlegging during the Prohibition Era,
running a ship across Lake Superior. He gained neither wealth

nor fame in this illegal venture. Family stories relate that my father was missing in action for four months on one of his runs. Chances are that he was nabbed by one of Eliot Ness's agents and did time in an American hoosegow.

Poverty, the Depression, hard work, the loss of his first wife who died in childbirth, and being a widower with four boys and no family roots in America took its toll. Three and a half years after my mother's death, my father died of chronic myocarditis on June 29, 1944. He lived forty years and twenty days.

Our parents left us naked and our love bruised and beaten because they died. Each of us manifested our emotions differently—anger, loss, fantasy, and indifference. It would take years to confront this family tragedy and come to a realization that we were not to blame. It was the damn gene pool.

In twenty days, we suddenly and tearfully traveled from Los Angeles, California, to Utica, New York.

When orphans are created, adults appear. Their motives may be charitable, a hand of God, of guilt, or of a praying mantis eager to devour the lesser and unsuspecting. From out of nowhere, a legal guardianship was established in the California courts replete with a court-appointed attorney. My brothers and I did not know our newly appointed guardian or his lawyer.

Upon my father's death, the authorities were at a loss as to where to place four orphaned boys aged four to fourteen years. Placement options were presented to the court. "Let's place them with the family." Fortunately or unfortunately, "the family" resided in Canada. Eliminate the "family" idea. Next, "Let's place them in the Masonic Home in West Covina, California." Fortunately or unfortunately, our father was a Freemason from Buffalo, New York, and never demitted to a California lodge. Eliminate the "West Covina" thought.

Another novel concept: "Let's place them for adoption." Fortunately, my fourteen-year-old brother said, "Hell, no." No Boys Town for us. Finally, "Let the legal guardian assume physical custody of the boys, after all, he is a Mason." The guardian respectfully declined the court. He demurred. "Send the boys to the New York Masonic Home and leave the father's estate in California." As always, the praying mantis would claim four more victims—this time with a legal guardian and a lawyer, with the blessings of the court.

We crossed the continental United States by steam locomotive. I remembered the Pullman cars. My two oldest brothers slept in the top bunk while Jim and I bunked down below. We were chaperoned by our legal guardian, Elmer Juckett, and another adult. (Remember, orphans have that effect of attracting adults.) Years later, my brother Jim told me that the other adult was the actor Melvyn Douglas. I don't have a clue why he accompanied us other than he was an adult.

We arrived in Utica on July 18, 1944. That day was my brother Chuck's fifteenth birthday and one day before my mother's would-be thirty-fourth birthday. July 18, 1944, was my other birthday; the day of a new emotional DNA that would identify me for the rest of my life.

After a couple of days of medical quarantine and tests, we were driven up to the camp. I don't ever recall seeing a pine tree, let alone thousands that stood as sentinels along the road. My trees were orange, lemon, avocado, loquat, and fig. I was frightened beyond belief and held on frantically to my brothers, seeking comfort and refuge. My brothers stared out of the car windows as we drove deeper into the Adirondack forest.

At midmorning we arrived at the camp and were greeted by a grandparent-like couple. "Call me Mr. Wiley," he stated.

"And this lady is Mrs. Wiley. We are in charge of everyone and everything." Each of us was assigned a permanent lot number in the Book of Orphans, Volume III. My number was 881. To my utter distress and fear, the separation of brothers occurred. My two oldest brothers were dispatched to the "barn." They were my surrogate parents for the past three years. My brother next in age went in another direction; where, I did not know. I was escorted, screaming, stuttering, and bawling to the nursery. This was my third painful experience of family separation in four years. No explanation was given except "This is the way things are done around here."

The nursery was located behind a row of pine trees in front of the lake. It was attached to a larger building called the dining hall, which had a building similar to the nursery attached on the other side. The three buildings were painted white with forest-green tin roofs, each with multiple window panes in front. All together, the trio of buildings gave the appearance of a very large white-and-green winged insect.

Ascending the concrete steps, turning right, I entered my new parentless home. There were about eight or nine children either older or younger milling about, playing with dolls, teddy bears, or building blocks. I don't remember any of them smiling or being hyper as children usually are. I was on my own, like it or not.

I wandered out to the porch area in the window-encased front of the building. There I spotted a swarthy child about my age with the darkest eyes playing with tin soldiers. I held up my left arm with my hand cupping the back of my head to keep the swarthy child from witnessing my sobbing and stuttering. He heard me, declared a temporary armistice in his warfare, and stated, "Hi, I'm Johnny. Do you want to be the Americans or the Germans?"

I didn't know what a German was. I was from California, but I knew who Japanese were and that we were at war with Japan. I knew that our neighbors down the street in San Diego were forcibly removed from their home in 1942. I retorted, "I'm K-k-ken-ny. Doo-doo y-you wa-wanna be the 'Mericans or the Japs?

At that moment, over tin-soldier war, I met a new brother. He was not, as my California experience thought, a Mexican. Johnny was a Greek and my new brother.

While engaged in our metallic warfare, interchanging Germans for Japanese as the fallen enemy, leaving the Americans unscathed, I could hear a distant drumroll. There was a pause in the drums and then a command: "Salute, one!" Then the drumroll continued closer and louder. My thoughts were that that these drumbeats only made our war games more realistic.

Suddenly, Johnny jumped up and ran to the window and in stride told me, "The big kids are coming, we're going to have lunch!"

Confused and frightened, I too ran to the window. As the drummers turned right at the end of the row of pine trees with the big kids marching behind from tallest to shortest, a fight broke out between two big kids. It didn't take me long to spot one of the combatants. My brother Chuck was fighting with a stocky, curly-headed boy. The other big kids broke up the brawl, and order was restored.

The big kids were big boys and big girls. I never saw so many boys and girls in one spot before. Once again, I began to stutter, "Whooo are th-these b-boys 'n girrrls?"

We were ushered into the dining hall from the white-and-green right wing to the white-and-green thorax. The nursery kids were directed to sit and dine on the raised stage of the dining hall. From that vantage, I saw that boys and girls were segregated by age and gender. I looked for my brothers in this crowded yet expansive room.

I spied both Chuck and Bob seated together with other older boys. I ran off the stage, made a beeline for them, and jumped onto Chuck's lap. Attempts by the "charity plantation" boss to return me to my proper seat were rebuffed by both brothers with a third who would bite the boss's ankles. The boss, not wanting to instigate another big-kid melee, relented. The boss must have gone on vacation. I sat in my brothers' laps for two more weeks.

I asked Chuck who he was fighting. He scowled. "Some wop."

"What's a wop?" I asked again.

"You know, Kenny, a dago, a greaseball, an *eye-talian,*" Chuck retorted.

I didn't know those words.

Hours later my first day at the camp ended. My head was buried in the pillow, sobbing and wanting for my brothers. I couldn't remember my parents.

A wop? I have two new brothers—a Greek and an Italian. My emotional DNA was beginning a dramatic transformation on July 18, 1944.

Separation

The most powerful, fearful, and harshest word coming in, going out, and in between at the Home was *separation*. You came in being separated from a parent or both. The circumstances were beyond your control, but you were saddened or felt guilt nevertheless. The circumstances were never fully explained or understood. Worse yet, the sadness or guilt was never addressed. You simply had to cope with a very complex issue. And you left separated from your second family. I don't believe it was ever the intention of the Home's administration to explain or assist you with the issue of separation.

Upon admission, you were issued a number. Your name, your date of birth, your parents' names, your father's Masonic lodge affiliation, and your religious denomination were entered into the Book of Orphans. You were sent to the hospital for a cursory medical examination, and two days later, you entered the segregated population of kids. Older siblings went to the place where other older siblings lived, either boy or girl. Young ones of tender years regardless of gender went to the nursery. You were officially separated, and you continued in that living arrangement until the day you left.

I entered the Home at a tender age of four years. When our mother died, my two eldest brothers, Chuck and Bob, served as the surrogate parents to my brother Jim and me. They taught me to talk and walk. They changed my diapers and babysat me in a motherless home. They played and laughed with me while holding their own sorrows within. They fed me in the morning and put me to bed at night. They taught me to swim and took me to the San Diego Zoo, which was a block away from our house. All that ended when our father died. We entered the Home and became separated.

Upon admission, there was no counseling administered or advice given as to your new surroundings—your new life. It never occurred to those in charge that you came as damaged goods and were in need of repair. You had to fix things yourself or do the best you could. I don't believe there was anyone qualified within the administration who could offer meaningful assistance or guidance. Instead, rules would suffice as your guide. There were no houseparents or mentors. There were only matrons and patrons. This rule-laden arrangement was reinforced on a daily basis by mass feeding, identical clothing, and on-time uniform activities and practices. In some twisted, ironic way, as you came more and more separated from your former life and natural siblings, you began to coalesce with other children and coexist with the new rules. I embraced the former but was ill at ease with the latter.

Those living parents who placed their children in the Home were forbidden to visit them for three months after placement. Perhaps this was the administration's plan for "final separation" from parental influence. One father was seen looking through the wrought iron fence along the Bleeker Street boundary in search of his children. He did this on a weekly basis after driving a distance of two hundred miles each way. Finally, his resolve gave way to the weekly driving grind, not to mention the cost of travel and lodging and the toll on his emotions. This form of separation was more akin to the *final solution* than a logical plan of placement in a caring children's home.

Being unable to live physically closer to my older brothers in essence denied me recollections of my early childhood years and the relationship I had with my parents. I never got to ask the simple questions that a curious child would inquire: What was our mother's favorite color? Did she miss Grandma still in Canada? What did she and Daddy do for fun? Who did she like best? Where did Daddy work? Did he take you guys fishing? Where did I learn to speak Spanish? Why did Mommy and Daddy die? Are they in heaven? These childish questions languished, and then time eroded their sentimental value until they finally slipped away unnoticed and unanswered. My separation from the past was completed.

I never knew of siblings being roommates despite their cultural or preadolescent patterns. It seemed to me that brothers rooming together would be natural, even if there was a disparity in ages. For some unknown colossal blunder, this fraternal event never took place. When I became older, I was told by one of the girls that they were never roommates. Charlotte and Mary were twins. They entered the Home at twelve years of age together with their older brother Carl. The brother, naturally, was sent to Wiley Hall, where the older boys resided. By nature's act, one of the twins began her menstrual period while the other was still in prepuberty. Those in authority opined that the menstruating twin live with the older girls and the other be separated to the younger. The administration completed a successful but idiotic mitosis of twins.

The only time I was able to capitalize on separation was after my eldest brother, Chuck, voluntarily left the Home to join the US Navy in 1945 and, in 1947, my second brother, Bob, also voluntarily left to join the US Air Force. Neither brother really liked the Home much. They were old enough to figure out the system and wanted out. Strangely, each joined a rule-laden organization. However, each liked the idea of a meager paycheck and the opportunity for promotion—something that the Home did not offer.

My third brother, Jim, wanted to assume the big-brother role with great eagerness, sometimes to my detriment. He was too damn fussy and picky as to what I should and should not do. My refusals and stubbornness only went so far. He would become frustrated and would threaten to punish me. I had been in the Home long enough to know that there was no militia to come to your aid. So I did the next best thing and told my brother that I would write to Chuck and tell him what was going on. At the time, Chuck was stationed on the island of Guam, a million miles away. It would take three weeks for a letter to go each way. Jim, fearing possible wrath from Chuck, was kept at bay for almost two months. By that time, things cooled off between my brother and me. Having a brother in the Pacific and another flying around the world to unknown places helped to create a modicum of harmony for the last two Pettit boys. I enjoyed a fear-free environment while my brother's environs were fraught with his anticipation of remote brotherly retribution.

While I created my own rules of engagement for a fear-free environment, my belief was that the Home went in an opposite direction. The administration created an environment of fear with its unwritten "get kicked out of the Home" mentality.

Discipline was expected from every individual working or living within the Home. If you violated any rule or policy, punishment was administered. The discipline was haphazard and tended to be on the harsh side. You were ordered to stand on one leg, to have your mouth taped shut, to crawl through the mill, to be paddled, or restrictions were placed on your activities and whereabouts. Discipline did not fit the violation. It was one size fits all. Discipline was not progressive but rather sudden and final, like a *guillotine*. The ultimate was being dismissed from living at the Home and to fend on your own.

What was stunning about this final solution was that it was done so dispassionately and with ease. Never mind the age of the violator or his fears about being separated from another family. Never mind about the feelings of those siblings left behind. Never mind about the feelings of the parent who went through unbearable hardship when placing the child within the protection of the Home. Never mind the future of the child kicked out of the Home. Never mind about the oath that the superintendent took concerning the welfare of widows and orphans. The rules were the rules no matter how arbitrary they were or disproportionate when meted out. There was no appeal process to a higher authority, or at least, we were never informed; and the superintendent's authority was never questioned or reviewed. He applied the *golden rule*. That is, he kept the gold and created the rules.

I believe that one of the rules included a dislike for Italian boys. One of my older brothers, an Italian boy by the name of Leo, had a like for the superintendent's daughter. This did not go well with the superintendent, despite the fact that another Home boy, an Anglo, had an identical like for his younger daughter. For following a natural act of liking a girl, Leo was kicked out of the Home and the Anglo kid stayed, eventually marrying the sup's younger daughter. I'm sure Leo was perplexed and angered by this act of discrimination. I'm sure his younger brother, Matty, was just as perplexed and angry. Those feelings didn't matter. Each boy would have to go on alone; each victimized by a senseless and selfish rule.

If only the Home took time to talk with us about the pain we all harbored, attempted to understand our confusion, listened to our fears, encouraged our desires, or said "I love you" or asked us about our parents, our favorite color, asked anything rather than invoking the rules, then *separation* would have been the war between the states and not a word to fear.

Nursery Days

The nursery was one of two residences on the other side of the main road at the Masonic Home. The other was the superintendent's residence. He was the person in charge of the overall goings-on at the Home. Each operation or building had an in-charge person. There was an in-charge person for the old folks residing in the Vrooman Building, one each for Wiley Hall, the boiler room, the Soldiers and Sailors Memorial Hospital, the Knights Templar Building, the garage, the bakery, the laundry, the maintenance shops, the infirmary, the groundskeepers and the night watchmen. The only place that lacked an in-charger was the cemetery. Either no one wanted the job or the last buried was temporarily in charge until the next *stiff* was planted. Counting the headstones, the cemetery had the most in-charge people.

Living on the "other side of the road" in 1945 with the superintendent as a neighbor did not have its privileges. The in-charge person at the nursery was like many of the others, especially those who were selected as matrons for children. Miss Manna was young, single and somewhat attractive. She was, however, intolerant of children. I guess this qualified her to be a person in charge of children of tender years. Our welfare was dependent on her mood and the presence or absence of her boyfriend, a US Navy sailor. While he was on leave, Miss Manna was the "welfare queen." The two spent much of their time together necking in the downstairs parlor. While her sailor boy was on duty, Miss Manna was the "wicked witch." I had hoped the war would end soon.

The nursery building was a two-story colonial redbrick structure with white columns supporting a portico at the front entry. A glass-enclosed sunporch extended the entire southeast side of the residence, allowing for warm mornings. Across the main road from the sunporch was the Daniel D. Tompkins Memorial Chapel, dedicated in 1911. This New England-style chapel with its white steeple and its iconic four columns was a nondenominational house of worship. Its brick walls were Puritan New England. However, its austerity was counterbalanced with magnificent stained-glass windows portraying various biblical myths and heroes, with "Faith, Hope and Charity" as the Tiffany triumvirate. Its glass ceiling hosted the heaven's constellations. The insides were to enrich the spiritual needs of Christians, Jews and anyone else who sought to be uplifted.

Behind the nursery was an expansive lawn studded with elm trees claimed by the squirrels, chipmunks, and various birds. The trees provided the much-needed shade during the hot and humid summer months as well as wind breaks during the bitter cold and blustery winter season. The lawn and trees were our playground with daily restrictions imposed by the queen witch.

The first floor of the nursery, in addition to the parlor, contained a library, a dining room, a kitchen, and a storage room for tricycles, wagons, baby buggies, and an assortment of toys. The matron's living quarters also occupied the ground floor. The second floor was primarily dormitory rooms and a large multistalled bathroom. The main dormitory room was above the sunporch. There was a cellar. It was a coal cellar.

When I arrived at the Home in 1944, there were eight boys and girls residing in the nursery. The boys were dressed in short pants with knee-high stockings. On Sundays we wore the short pants, stockings, a dickey with coat and tie. A white handkerchief was neatly tucked into each breast pocket. The girls wore print dresses with knee-high stockings, and an exaggerated bow was tied in their hair. All of us were neatly coiffed and plastered with hair oils. We comprised the class of 1940-1944.

Louise was the oldest at eight years of age, followed by Sammy, "Butch," Lawson, Georgie V., George K., myself, Johnny V., and Barbara K., the youngest at age four. Some of the nursery kids had older siblings also residing at the Home, such as George K., who had three older sisters, "Butch" with an older brother, and me with three older brothers. Having older siblings at the Home was a benefit. They served as the last link to your former life and were your benefactor-in-residence and, sometimes, your court of last resort. As the months and years passed by, the older siblings played lesser roles as you melded into the social routines at the Home. Sammy and Lawson moved to Panama to be with their mother. I never saw these brothers again.

At times, I felt that we were mere window dressing for the Home's image and administration. We were often photographed as a group, clutching a doll or teddy bear. Our grim faces were representations of inner feelings of loneliness, being parentless, and lack of filial love. We posed with war veterans at Christmas, with Masons on St. John's Day, or in the holy shrine across the main road. What could make a better sell than orphans receiving the bounty from America's best?

This window dressing served to enrich the cult of the individual that stood for nearly forty years at the Home. William J. "Pop" Wiley was an icon among the pantheon of Masons of New York State. Much of the construction of buildings dedicated to the needs of the orphans was made during his tenure. He was committed to the welfare of the children, ensuring that they attended public schools, received home economics training, clothing, toys, and spiritual guidance. He was much photographed, filmed, and his deeds chronicled. In appreciation of "Pop" Wiley's birthday, the nursery kids rehearsed and orated the following greeting:

Happy Birthday with Our Love
To Mr. Wiley from the Nursery

Hickory, dickory dock, the mouse ran up the clock,
The clock struck Nineteen Forty-five
And the prayers said in 1910 are still alive.
God Bless Mamma Wiley, God Bless Papa Wiley.

"Now I Lay Me Down to Sleep," said on battlefields and
briny deep,
Little prayers and big ones, no two just alike,
Your boys and girls, who you remember when each child
was a little tike,
On this your birthday, in loving thoughts, around you
meet.

A million thanks they say and ask God to give you
    strength anew
To carry on the work you have done, for them and others
    yet to come
We wish you all the very best life holds,
With health and happiness as the year unfolds."

No one had received greater attention. He was the number 1 in-charge man.

The in-charge matron of the nursery did not receive attention or recognition for her energies, which were usually negatively charged. Miss Manna was a disciplinarian of the first order. She believed that children were not to be heard or seen. She would not hesitate to tape a child's mouth shut in order to maintain silence. George K. feared retribution if he revealed his mouth-taping incident. Standing on one leg for great lengths of time was standard punishment. In addition to her penchant for punishment, Miss Manna had some weird edicts for proper child health care. At least once a day, all of us were required to sit on the toilet and not to depart until we experienced a bowel movement. We would sit on the toilet for a seemingly extended and exhaustive time, with legs dangling and stomachs convulsing in order to "dump." If you were successful, you cried out, "Miss Manna, I made a BM!" The witch would actually enter the bathroom stall and inspect your excremental success.

I don't know how or what a child does to merit punishment that requires a five-year-old to stand on one leg for an interminable amount of time. There was no penal law that could describe such an act or its inappropriate judgment. Well, Johnny V. and I managed to somehow violate Miss Manna's ironclad rules. Neither Johnny nor I could recall the offending act. As punishment, we were sent to the toy room and ordered to stand on one leg. A minute and thirty seconds is a long time for a child. It ranked right up there with "Are we there yet?" in terms of elapsed time. In any event, we became tired and dared to grasp hold of the handlebars of a tricycle. We got caught. The queen was out, but the witch was in.

She grabbed us both by an arm and marched us down to the cellar—the coal cellar. She turned out the lights and locked the door. I'm sure that Johnny and I did not know the difference between heaven and hell despite the white chapel across the road. Within seconds we had a darn good idea what hell was like. We couldn't see beyond our noses, let alone one another. We felt instant fear and began to cry, then broke into uncontrollable sobbing. We stumbled about, tripping over random coals, reaching out into blackness, and finally finding one another still sobbing.

"I'm scared, Kenny, and I don't know where my brother Georgie is," Johnny uttered between sobs. "I'm so scared," Johnny plaintively cried.

"So-so am I, J-J-Johnny," I stuttered as a felt his face in the coal-black cellar. Tears and snot were freely running down his cheeks and nose. It took forever for us to catch our breaths and bring our sobbing down to whimpering.

I remembered my brothers who lived in Wiley Hall, the boys' building on the other side of the road two hundred yards away. *They can help me; they always did. But where is Wiley Hall? I've never been there.* I remember while playing under the elm trees, I could see some big boys mingling about in front of a three-story brick building. *That must be Wiley Hall.*

We could see dim light coming through the ground-level cellar windows. That would be our escape route. I boosted

Johnny up, and he managed to unlock the window. We crawled out, looking rather grimy, and darted through the elm trees, zigzagging our way to Wiley Hall.

If the coal cellar was hell, then Wiley Hall must have been purgatory. I never saw so many big boys in one place. With our blackened faces coursed with streams of snot and tears, I believe that we took them off guard. They thought Johnny and I were two devilish pranksters on the lam from the nursery. We were on the lam, but we were on a mission of mercy—ours.

The three stories of Wiley Hall were graded by age. The first floor was occupied by ten- to twelve-year-old kids, the second floor comprised the thirteen- and fourteen-year-olds, while the third floor was reserved for the really big kids. Gaining access to the top floor was like running the gauntlet. As you ascended the staircase, the kids got bigger and bolder. I ran into my eleven-year-old brother, Jim. He wouldn't do. I needed my two oldest brothers. They were my surrogate parents. I asked Jim where Bob and Chuck were, and he responded, "Third floor."

As Johnny and I were dashing up the staircase like two runaway juvenile slaves, I could hear odd names being called and shouted at: "Hey Shorty, Jake, Ghost, Rock Head, Ape, Smitty, Matty—you guys seen the Pettits?"

"Third floor" came in a chorus of responses.

I saw the Italian guy my brother got into a fight with at my first day at the Home. I walked quietly by him staring at the black-and-white checkered linoleum floor. He gave way and watched Johnny and me pass by.

Finally, top floor. I cried out for my brothers. I could hear "Down here, Kenny. Whadda ya doin' here? What the hell happened to you! Who's the other kid?"

As I approached my oldest brother Chuck's room, a giant walked out. He was huge, wearing thick eyeglasses and possessing hands the size of a baseball-catcher's mitt. He peered down at us and bellowed, "Hi there, little fellas." He also was wearing a smile from ear to ear.

My brother said, "Hey, Sears, this is my little bud, Kenny."

After seeing the giant smiling, I relaxed and told my brother what had happened to Johnny and me. The sobbing started all over again. The giant knelt down and assured me that everything would be all right. I felt better.

Chuck got Bob and both gently held Johnny's and my hands as we marched back to the nursery. Once inside, the two of us scampered into the sunporch. It was light outside, and the warmth of the sun removed the chill of fear. I could hear shouting, arguing, and threats of great bodily harm to Miss Manna as well as to her "Popeye" sailor if he ever got shore leave again. I don't remember seeing either the queen or the witch ever again. It became more fun playing with my eight brothers and sisters.

The nursery was a red brick building that was cold as stone. It was not a home.

Obedience

The first lesson you learned when you entered the Home was obedience. Each activity and behavior was performed in proper sequence. No deviations were permitted, and you were not expected to inquire of or seek special favors. Life and living were too orderly. It was spoken or written and never discussed.

You arose from the bed at the same time, bathed and brushed your teeth at the same time, dressed in nearly identical clothing, and sat for meals in unison. You boarded the big blue bus with the title Masonic Home emboldened on each side. When nearing our destination, most of us would duck below the window level to save us from looking conspicuous.

My summertime was spent at the camp, an idyllic spot in the southern Adirondack Mountains. No matter the friendliness of the pines, lake, and rustic cottages, conformity persisted. We would rise at the same time to the call of a bugle. We marched in military fashion—tallest to the shortest, boys followed by girls, and led by a drum corps on our way to the dining hall. The march was briefly interrupted by our honoring of Old Glory under the watchful eye of the superintendent.

Summer activities were organized and, for the most part, enjoyable. However, every activity was governed by the clock or bugle. Don't ignore time, bugle blasts, or the marching formation, or you had hell to pay. Some form of punishment was meted out for the slackers. The acceptable excuses were illness, a rare visit from a blood relative, or rain. God, I used to pray for rain just to break up the monotony or go fishing.

Fishing on a rainy day did not give you redemption from obedience. It merely exempted you from wearing khaki pants and a striped T-shirt and marching to the dining hall. You were still conditioned to respond Pavlovian to the damn bugle calls and get your butt in line. Many times, we would attempt to bribe the bugler to blow "Gabriel's horn" a few minutes later in order to give us a jump start. There were three bugle calls. First, an alert. Second, get going, and third, marching formation is two minutes away. It was always a challenge to make a mad dash from the trout stream a mile away or row a boat from across the lake, dress, and be in formation from the first clarion call.

Sundays at the camp were rather angelic. Instead of khakis, we wore white pants, a T-shirt, and a white sweatshirt if needed. The mornings were spent sweeping pine needles off all walkways, only for the needles to fall back down during the ensuing week. After the usual march to lunch, we had to rest before chapel. Hell's bells, I never understood the rest period. It wasn't like we were about to launch into a Wagnerian opera. Chapel services were simple and dull. I could only think of the trout stream while the "spirit of poof" wafted through the pine rafters.

Most of us were athletic. We had to know how to swim. There was a swimming beach with a floating dock about one hundred feet anchored offshore. The dock had a lifeguard tower perched high up with two lifeguards patrolling the perimeter of the swimming area. There was also a roped-off area for the human minnows learning to swim. There was a rule that you could not jump, dive, or be pushed off the back of the dock. To my knowledge, the depth of the water in back was the same as in front. I guess that was the "no eyes in the back of your head" rule.

Life was governed according to rules. Independent thought was not encouraged and was actually frowned upon. That's how the administration kept a check on the boys and girls. Curiosity and exploration took a backseat to obedience and conformity. I wasn't very good with the commands of heel, fetch, and sit. As a result, I was often found in the doghouse.

In Wiley Hall, the boys' dormitory in Utica, there was a bulletin board posted on the wall halfway down the hall on the first floor. The postings were of the month's movies, which member of the old folks had passed away, which Masonic lodge was coming for a visit, and a new regulation neatly typed and signed by William T. Clark, superintendent. Of course the movies were important. Cowboys, pirates, and knights received rave reviews from the boys. The girls enjoyed love stories and musicals. If you knew one of the departed, there was a brief moment of silence. We could care less about who was visiting. Just don't give us that line, "Oh, you poor thing. Wouldn't you like to come and live with us?" Our silent retort was, "Why the hell would I want to live with you? I don't even know you, and besides, I lost one family and I'm not about to lose another!"

What grabbed my attention were the neatly typed and autographed rules and regulations. They were arbitrary and without foundation. "Don't go on the farm." "Refrain from inviting city kids to the Home." "No sledding down cemetery hill." "Do not swim in the pool at night." I read these rules with rapt attention and silently questioned the wisdom of these dicta. These prohibitions were my playground. They served not to take the kids' lives away but rather take the lives out of the kids. I had the gall to muse, *Nobody asked me about this rule.* What's a swimming pool for? Why can't I play baseball with a city kid on our diamond? Sledding down cemetery hill was childhood mayhem where nobody got hurt. The farm was where we perfected our hunting prowess.

My days in the doghouse became more frequent as new rules were published and posted. I was willing to take the risk. Most of my brothers and sisters conformed. I couldn't blame them. They were right.

Scoom-Bah-Dee

E mbarrassment at the Home came early and often. It was etched in stone, and it was ingrained in our experiences. You carried it with you, and you never forgot its impacts. It was a state of mind and was being brought upon by conformity and confinement. The administration of the Home expected the kids to be dependent upon the largess of their beneficence and not exercise freedom of movement or thought and certainly not to be influenced by any outside people, ideas, or forces. Their thought was that they provided food, shelter, and clothing. These were the basic human needs. Anything more would be excessive and unnecessary.

Scoom-bah-dee is a phonetic southern Italian dialect for embarrassment. It derives from the word *imbarrazzo*, but its etiology has become lost in regional linguistic dialogues. It was a word used by the Italian population of east Utica and spoken in the public schools. Naturally, the word migrated into the Home boys' lexicon by way of assimilation in school and proximity to the Italian neighbors. It was never declared a forbidden word by the administration, but it was frowned upon whenever its use was declared in open conversation. Hence, it became one of those words cached in our vocabulary and derisively used in casual conversation.

When my brothers and I arrived at the Home, we were issued clothing that was remarkably similar to those worn by the other boys. While in the nursery, I wore knickers with knee-length stockings, a blousy shirt, and a floppy large bow tie. The older boys wore striped T-shirts with khaki pants. The girls were similarly clad in bib overalls and blouses for informal dress. Skirts were worn well below the knees, with white blouses. During our summer months at the camp, we marched in military fashion, complemented by a drum corps, to the dining hall. We wore the T-shirt/khaki combo and bib overalls during the week, and on Sundays we dressed in white T-shirts and trousers. (I assumed there was some chaste relationship of the color white with Sundays.) In other words, we were in constant uniform.

This preordained dress code was for conformity and, no doubt, cheaper when bought by the lot. So early on, being unique in dress was not encouraged. We were to wear dungarees when at play or leisure. Levi's were verboten. None was to stand out in the crowd. We were to all look alike wherever we were. This was especially evident when we went to high school. The blue bus with the identification of Masonic Home Utica New York emboldened on it sides would empty its human cargo of boys and girls who all dressed alike. It didn't take long for the students to declare, "Here comma da masonica homa kids." Ironically, we did stand out in the crowd. This identification of sameness was embarrassing. It was scoom.

To avoid this sameness, the boys would inquire prior to departing on the blue bus as to which colored T-shirt was to be worn that day, even though the striped patterns were identical.

We avoided being seen together so as not to draw unwarranted attention to ourselves. We walked on opposite sides of the hallways, took different stairwells and floors, and seldom ate together in the school's cafeteria.

The beginning of each academic semester would be another cause for embarrassment. Students would rent their textbooks on the first day of class. They would pay cash or promise to bring in the money the next day. This was the protocol. However, this did not apply to the "masonica homa kids." The teacher would announce, when your name was called, that you would be excused from payment because you were from the Masonic Home. We were different not in a positive light but rather in the shadows of being on the dole. This was embarrassing. This was scoom.

Much of the Masonic Home's property was framed by a seven-foot-high wrought iron fence. It ran along Bleeker Street, turned south, and meandered through the wooded area that separated the Home from the city of Utica. Other manmade barriers were linked with the wrought iron fence that completed the perimeter around the Home. These barriers gave the appearance of an institution to outsiders. It was the place where same-shirted kids lived. There were no Welcome signs at the entrances. This was an enclave for different people.

We were not encouraged to bring our friends, the city kids, to the Home. They were outsiders, maybe Catholics, or worse yet, Italians. For some unexplainable and unwritten reason, there appeared to be a prohibition about extending an invitation to these people. The prohibition, under certain circumstances, worked both ways. Once, I had received an invitation from a high school classmate, Charlie Digiorgio, to spend Sunday dinner at his home. I related to Charlie that the Home didn't welcome these acts of kindness with open arms. He assured me that the invitation was extended by his family and that Sunday dinner in an Italian household would be a memorable feast. His father showed up at the Home to formally extend the invitation. Mr. Digiorgio showed up in his finest suit with fedora in hand. With his head slightly bowed and in halting English, he politely sought permission for "Kenni Petti" to join him and his family for Sunday dinner. His gentlemanly request was summarily denied without explanation. I missed out on the best *antipasto and spaghetti* dinner ever. Worse yet, I would have to face Charlie at school on Monday. That was embarrassing. That was scoom.

Perhaps the capstone of misled awareness and sensitivity was the inscription atop the entry of the Administration Building, the nerve center of the Home's business, policy, and rule making mill. In bold letters chiseled into the sandstone slab were Masonic Home and asylum for children. My god, how could a kid explain a nineteenth-century pejorative word to a twentieth-century progressive world! This Dickensian appellation served the charitable purposes of Masonry but did us no favors. Those few city kids who did come and visit would stand and stare in disbelief at this inscription. They were convinced that Home Kids were different and should be treated with some skepticism. "Woodchuck" related how his schoolmates believed that the Home was an institution for juvenile delinquents and crazies. They weren't too far off about the delinquency but were led far astray about the crazies. As long as the Administration Building stood, it would be a source of personal embarrassment for many of us.

St. John's Day was *the* day in Masonry. It fell in late June just after school ended. For us, it was the harbinger of summer camp. To prepare for this day, the kids spent countless hours and weeks rehearsing songs by Gershwin, Berlin, Rogers and Hart, and Hammerstein. In addition, John Phillip Souza's marches were played endlessly until our lips and fingertips were calloused. On the last weekend in June, Masons from throughout New York descended upon the Home's grounds. Busloads from Kings and Queens (and the kids would say "Jacks" and "Aces") unloaded Masons, Eastern Star women, Knights Templar, Shriners, Tall Cedars of Lebanon, and any other mystics and "Grand Poo Bahs" from the East. The kids were up for display. Masonry would now behold its beneficence.

Other than singing Broadway music and thumping "Washington Post," the boys would be directed to stand by their rooms for the annual inspection and cheek-squeezing by Masons and their wives. Scores of couples would walk down the hallway of Wiley Hall, stop, and gaze into our rooms. As we stood outside our rooms, we would be asked how we liked living in the Home. We would politely demur and respond, "Oh, we like the Home very much. Would you like to see my room?"

Our responses were remote and insincere. The Home was the Home, not our home.

We knew it would come, and we dreaded the scene.

"Oh, you poor dear, you lost your parents. Wouldn't you like to come and live with us? We have a boy just about your age. He's someone you can play with."

Our responses were silent outrages. *Why the hell would I want to live with you? I didn't lose my parents. They died and that's why I'm here. I have a new family. Why would I want to leave my family again just to live with you and to play with your boy?*

They didn't get it. The men with lapel pins and rings, fezzes, swords, and plumed hats were oblivious to our feelings and experiences. It was all about them and their largess. The boys and girls were merely recipients and should act accordingly. This was embarrassing. This was scoom-bah-dee.

The Tonys

Perhaps the most venerable institution in the Home was the Tonys. Because of what they built, planted, mowed, raked, shoveled, cemented, painted, and endured, these men were an institution within an institution. The Tonys were the human Vatican toiling within the walls of the Masonic "Rome." They went about their labors with stoicism and earthly calm. Buildings were erected, lawns planted, trees blossomed, walkways laid, graves dug, and flowers placed with quiet dignity. Winters were less harsh and summers less oppressive because of these sons of Italy.

I never knew where the name "the Tonys" derived. Several years after I entered the Home, I was told that the men who went about their work were the Tonys. As I matured and became aware of ethnicity among my brothers and sisters, the stain of being Italian within the Home was no more manifested than the pejorative label affixed to the laborers who toiled. They were Italians, hence, the title "*the Tonys*." I guess they could have been called the Alfredos, Gustavos, Leopoldos or, for that matter, the Wopos. I wondered if the administration ever considered calling these gentlemen builders, creators, or even dreamers.

The Tonys' leader was Tomoso Yacovella. I remember Signore Yacovella as a quiet, hardworking, and dignified man who spoke directly to his crew in their native language. My brother Tom was named after his grandfather and was somewhat reticent about the relationship. The Tonys were plebeian; the Home's administration was patrician. My brother Tom never forgot that distinction. Whenever they crossed paths, the elder gave a reassuring nod to his grandson. My brother smiled and gained confidence.

Signore Yacovella's American beginnings were his arrival from Italy and settlement in Utica. He was a goat herder in his native land and was accustomed to being close to the earth. Upon settling in the New World and beginning his new family, the *signore* realized that getting a job was essential for living the American dream. He bought a bicycle and pedaled to the Home and applied for employment. William "Pop" Wiley, the architect/landscaper with a vision, did not hesitate in hiring the new Italian immigrant. For over half a century, this gentleman created the arboreal and garden splendor of the Masonic Home and Asylum.

How ironic it was, for the Tonys' *salotto* was located directly beneath the superintendent's office in the Administration Building. It was here in the basement of the cavernous gothic building that the Tonys would convene for work assignments, talk about Joe DiMaggio, and speak as *fratelli*. Their wooden straight-back chairs were situated in a triangle so that the men could look at one another with the *signore* at the apex. Some of the boys would spy and listen in on their conversations, which were punctuated with frenetic hand gestures and utterances. It was opera without a balcony. We didn't understand a word of it. Maybe Tom did, but he didn't let on out of respect for his grandfather.

They drank their strong *cafe*, smoked their foul-smelling *sigaros*, and trudged off to work.

They pushed their lawn mowers across the expansive lawns, used scythes on Garage Hill, and manicured the baseball diamond. Perhaps the great DiMaggio would come and play ball here.

"Who is that guy?" queried Bernie.

Again, "Who is that guy sitting on the lawn mower? Kid Modern?"

Bernie was the master of turning the phrase or mimicking any sound. His inquiry was profound. "Kid Modern" was the first among the Tonys to be identified with operating mechanical equipment. For decades, grounds keeping and construction were done manually with blood and sweat. However, at the farm, John Deeres were employed for plowing, planting, and harvesting. Dan and Tony, the two draft horses that hauled the slop wagon, were retired to pasture long before the Tonys were mechanized.

I don't remember any of the Tonys working the fields. All the farmers hailed from the British Isles. The Tonys were destined to carry the stain not on their shirts but rather on their backs.

Humor

I f sadness was the ticket for entry, then the rides were free and somewhat dark. Life at the Home was both regimented and kinetic. Yes, there was a dress code, mandatory haircuts, prearranged music and choir lessons, don't miss a meal, get to bed on time, and rules upon rules. But there were also unwritten rules about simply having fun. The Home afforded the kids unlimited access to its expansive acreage, farm buildings, and the spooky sanctums of its gothic structures, all without permission. Who cared?

There were three kinds of fun. One was open, fair-minded, and with limitations. The other was hidden, made up on the spot, and knew no bounds. And the third was somewhere in between. Baseball was a shining example of the first, sneaking into the gothic basements was the second, and "elevator" baseball was the 'tweener. In all three, the "code" prevailed.

While engaged in all three endeavors, it was the second one that captured my attention and imagination. The ingredients for the success of number 2 (which, by the way, was how you usually ended up) were a skeleton key, the guts of a burglar, and the stupidity a doorknob.

Setting dirty clothes on an open bear trap was the ultimate for guts and stupidity. Dirty laundry certainly fell into the dress-code category, and the trap certainly qualified for the rules-upon-rules rule. This was the humor that was in vogue in my prior generation. The big boys would joyfully set the bait and trap in anticipation that Mr. Riley, the patron of the barn, would unwittingly dive into the impending disaster and heroically defend the rule.

The skeleton key was a generational thing. It was one of those hand-me-down practices. It was passing the torch in order to keep the Home Kid flame burning. My older brother Jim passed the skeleton key on to me. No doubt he was the recipient from some brother older than him. It was said that Leo was the king of the key. I'm sure if you traced the DNA of that key, it would date back to King Solomon. The key allowed me to form an ad hoc gang with the purpose of looting the basement of the Smith Infirmary. That basement was a treasure trove of booty fit for a pirate. Turn-of-the-century steamer trunks were neatly stored in the rooms. When opened, all kinds of riches were within grasp—watches, silver dollars, silks, *schlocky* jewelry, stamps, shoes, and corsets. Yes, number 2 got us. We did the crime within the time.

Another qualifier for the stupidity award was my ill-fated trip to one of the outbuildings on the farm. Three of us—two Home Kids and a city kid—headed for a building that housed the John Deere machinery with the intention of shooting starlings with our Daisy BB guns. We were plinking birds without regard to a bag limit when I had this dumb idea of plinking one of the boys and then making a mad dash for cover. I reached cover, peeked through a tiny opening, and *plink*, a BB found its mark into my left eye. A half-mile trek with snow packed on my eye ensued. When I was asked "What happened!" I made a one-eyed, tearful response, "I ran into a tree." (Remember, the code.) Thirty years later while reminiscing at a reunion, the superintendent once again inquired, "What happened?" Within a nanosecond, trying to recall a three-decade-old injury, I nonchalantly replied, "I ran into a tree." He didn't believe me thirty years ago, and he didn't believe me then. The guts of a burglar.

Perhaps a milder form of the hidden, made-up, no-limits humor was when Tom and I went off to check our traps on the edge of the forest that formed a wooded curtain around the camp's athletic field. For a few weeks, there were reports and sightings of wildcats in and around the camp. These reports and sightings would be our skeleton key. Two Home girls, Lillian and Gerry, were sauntering along a path on their way to a blueberry patch. Tom and I spied the girls and decided to take cover. As the girls walked several yards past us, I let out a bloodcurdling scream. The girls whirled around, bug-eyed and momentarily speechless, each trying to outpace the other in their escape from terror. Whizzing past in a cloud of pine needles, Tom and I fell apart with laughter. The older girl, Lillian, heard our laughter, turned about, and regained her ability to speak, no, yell. She let out four feet of cusswords that would have made a stevedore blush. The girls continued their rapid retreat into the arms of the patron of the boys. Over the hill and through the woods came bring-'em-back Frank Hall toting a .22-caliber rifle. Do we blame this on city kids? Nah.

Perhaps the most benign form of "number-2 humor" was the telling of Ethel about the existence of a lake smoother. While witnessing one of those Adirondack rainstorms with its sudden change, Ethel, a first-year Home Kid, remarked how smooth the lake appeared. That gave rise to invoke humor. One of the boys said that the lake was calm because of the smoother. Ethel took the bait. "What? Where?" The boys joined in chorus and pointed out the location of the fictitious smoother. "Take the path to Dell'armi's, keep going until you run into a shack. Stop there, enter but watch out for snakes and spiders. You will see a shaft sticking up through the floor with a handle. Turn the handle two turns to the left, three turns to the right, and one turn back, one turn to the left." By god, she got it. We had to explain the directions but once. Obediently, Ethel trudged off to the shack. A miracle! The lake smoothed out.

Not being totally satisfied with their ruse, the boys upped the ante and instructed Ethel to continue her assignment twice daily for the duration of the camp session. Ethel obliged until the superintendent's wife caught wind. Not possessing the same sense of humor as the boys, the assignment ceased, and the boys were chastised.

The 'tweener came on the last night at camp. Tradition dictated that there would be the annual pillow fight among the boys. Once taps was played and the lights turned off, the nocturnal game began. You had no idea who or what you were hitting. It didn't matter. No score was being kept. Soon, things erupted into a melee, and laughter hit a remarkable decibel level. I'm sure the bullfrogs at the White Bridge covered their nonexistent ears with their existing webbed feet. We asked for it. A blinding beam of light flashed on—on to the biggest butt in the cottage. As George and his big butt scrambled up to their top bunk, the flashlight holder, the superintendent's wife, exclaimed, "Why, George, the size of you!"

All in all humor, in any form, prevailed at the Home.

Labor and Employment

I was always fascinated by the division of labor and who got appointed to certain jobs and the criteria for selection. To my knowledge, there were no skills, knowledge, or agility tests for appointment. You didn't apply. You were told that this or that was your chore. Period. "Someone's got to do it" was the explanation. Jobs were not interesting, nor did they prepare you for the future, except keep your head down and keep working. In a sense, that was preparing for the future. Jobs tended to be menial, boring, and repetitious. The jobs the Home Kids had were reflective of the "age of industry." Cheap labor.

Most of the assignments were at the camp. I had the distinction of having dishwashing jobs at the camp and the Home. I was told, "It's in your blood, Kenny." My brothers Bob and Jim preceded me in the "pearl diving" business. Based upon the gene pool, I couldn't take to argument. Washing, busing, and busting dishes put $10 a month in my camp pockets and $5 in Utica. Dishwashing was a labor of love. It was creative and an act of caring. How can you argue with success?

The labor market was really at the camp. There was so much to do for so little wages. There were choice jobs, and then there were jobs that would foster "wildcat" strikes in an industrialized nation. The Home was neither a free market society nor a nation. It was a closed enclave where kids labored.

There were choice jobs, social jobs, meaningful jobs, yes-sir-boss jobs, and short-lived entrepreneurial jobs. Choice jobs were defined by their wages and their distance from dirt and grime. These jobs were the mailman and truck swamper. These were once-a-day, five-days-a-week jobs. Being a mailman was a commitment to walking short distances to pick up and deliver mail, taking short orders to buy candy at Woodgate. The mailman didn't walk to Woodgate. He rode in a car. The distance was not short. The defining criterion for these jobs was the ability to read. They received the princely stipend of $15 per month, plus tips for the mailman.

Those chosen worked at the Candy Shoppe (I never did figure out the spelling of this hangout) or the library. I had no idea what the pay was, but they were nice places to be. Ruthie got fired by Dr. Clark for allegedly serving more scoops of ice cream to the kids than the old folks. How does one get fired for serving ice cream to a kid? Old folks can get cranky when young folks can get happy. Personally, I enjoyed the library because of my early fascination with books, and I would get spoiled by older sisters.

The meaningful jobs were labor intensive and necessary. These tasks included hauling drinking water, ice, and wood to the various cottages by wheelbarrow or on your back. My oldest brother, Chuck, was an iceman who lugged blocks of ice throughout the camp. He was so proficient that the boys actually created a lyric about his labors. The August evenings at the camp would get a bit chilly, if not downright freezing.

It was a wonder that no one froze to death, especially the old folks. Toting the wood, lifting that water bottle, and firing up the Franklin stoves would keep us thawed out until dawn.

Lifting a water bottle to the top of a cooler was downright dangerous. I couldn't accomplish this feat until I was thirteen. Once, Larry had the jug slip from his grasp, much to his dismay. The jug fell to the floor and shattered, and he looked like he ran into a chain saw. No one envied the job of loading the cooler. Little kids were left parched until some big kid got thirsty.

The yes-sir-boss jobs were stoop labor, manning a broom or axe, and washing dishes. One didn't have to read to become proficient with these jobs. You instilled inner tolerance and never watched the clock. Perhaps it was administration's way of building character and preparing for the future. The Protestant ethic of hard work and keeping us out of mischief has something to say about "idle hands are the devil's workshop."

There was a crew of four to gather, wash, and stack dishes, glasses, cups, and the ever-present Oneida silverware. The dishes and cups were formed from fired clay and always were a challenge when busing them. No waiter or dishwasher who ever toted a stack of dishes went without failure. If a dish was broken, the head chef would bark out, "A wasted dish is like wasted food! You can't use it anymore." Of course, we never used the dish anymore, but I wasn't sure about the food.

In any event, to hide the evidence of broken dishes, our predecessors carved a slot in the wooden floor large enough to deposit the busted pieces. The pieces piled on the ground below. The dishwashers pondered about a team of archeologists digging up the ruins five thousand years hence—if upon discovering the broken shards of pottery, would they have concluded that a violent society roamed the grounds of Round Lake?

Finally, there were the entrepreneurial jobs. These were creative, short-lived, and quite lucrative. You could double a month's salary in one hour. Butch had the market cornered on the collection of newspapers. Uncounted editions of the *New York Times* (especially the Sunday edition) and the Utica *Observer-Dispatch* were delivered daily to the Home's residents. Unfortunately, magazines like the *National Geographic Magazine, Life,* and *Look* did not count. Butch would simply collect and store the newsprint in the basement of Wiley Hall. After months of collection (and just prior to spontaneous combustion), Butch would bundle them and notify the local rag man to come and pick them up. Butch was being paid by the weight (Remember *National Geographic*?) Once we caught wind of that, humor number 2 kicked in. We offered to help Butch for a cut of the action. To increase the weight, we gathered slate from the banks of Starch Factory Creek and stuffed them into the bundles. Increased weight translated to increased "action." No doubt, we risked being bit by the hand that fed us.

Talk about being entrepreneurial!

Our first day at camp was met with stoop labor. All the weeds along the shore of the swimming beach had to be pulled. It was the only time the girls did stoop labor. The weed pulling was easy. The sand was soft and the shore, narrow. The following days was the same pulling only at the baseball field. This time, the pulling was not easy. The ball field was an amalgamation of sods that would resist a tractor pull. Thank God, we only had to yank the sods that squatted in the base paths and the infield where the fielders patrolled. The rest of the infield and outfield was left to the whims of Mother Nature. As a result, the ball field was a virtual pinball machine. Ground balls turned into abrupt ninety-degree angles. It may have been our home field, but the laws of geometry applied equally to opposing teams. We prayed for strikeouts and fly balls.

Without doubt, the worst labor job was "woods." This was the one discriminatory word given to the task of untangling, chopping, sorting, and stacking pine trees that were the victims of Hurricane Hazel in October 1954. Hazel didn't follow the well-worn path of her prior sisters when howling up the Atlantic seaboard after ravaging through the Caribbean Islands and Florida. It took a left turn somewhere in the Carolinas, drove north through Virginia, North Carolina, Pennsylvania, New York, and on into Canada. The Adirondacks pines were twisted toothpicks. Hazel was one pissed-off lady.

For the next three years, a ragtag force of teenage boys (with the exception of the choice-job holders) toiled and sweated in the wooded spaghetti. It was tantamount to a World War I battleground. You made three feet of progress on the frontline. While your tour of duty lasted only two hours from Monday through Friday, it was the drudgery and monotony that wore you down. Like marching to the chow hall, your only excuse from "woods" was rain. Many supplications were offered to the rain gods.

Old Folks

O ne of the more salient and impressionable aspects of the Masonic Home was the existence of elderly folks. These people were retired Masons and their wives or widows and members of the Eastern Star who were in their twilight years. They gave up their worldly positions and came to retire in the Home. They numbered in the hundreds. Their primary residence was the John W. Vrooman Building, the largest residential structure at the Home. The sod for this building was broken in 1927, and the old folks took up residence in this four-story brick building in 1929. With the Great Depression close at hand, the Vrooman Building was a godsend to these retirees.

The old folks would stick fairly close to their monolithic coop, not wandering about the expansive grounds. Some feared they couldn't find their way home, some feared the kids, and others were content to sit in their rooms and stare out through the windows at those trying to find their way home. Looking at the building, I would fear going home. The place looked like a joint with its massive wings on each side of a four-pillared entrance, 150-plus steel-framed windows in the front, and an equal number in the rear overlooking a cornfield. Somewhat ahead of its time, the north and south ends of the wings contained internal ramps to allow for easier accessibility for the halt and lame.

Some of the unfortunate ones resided in the Soldiers and Sailors Memorial Hospital, guarded by the bronzed likeness of Lt. Orville P. Johnson, son of a grand master. Poor Orville was killed in action during World War I and forever stood at attention in full US Army uniform during winter storms, spring rains, and summer humidity. He also served as a spotter and roost for an assortment of birds. Those who resided in the hospital often found it to be their sole and last residence.

As the population of the Vroomanians grew and aged and the population of the boys declined, the married couples migrated to the upper two floors of Wiley Hall. Living one floor below the seniors and sharing a common dining hall, the boys became well acquainted with them. The arrangement was living history. It was like someone in authority arranged a grandparental "adoption." This mix of septuagenarians and teenagers was not an interruption of our lives but rather a reason to fill in our idle time.

These senior citizens came from all walks of life—medicine, art, money, military, labor, education, and just plain folk. Many had fought in the trenches in France during World War I. Some would relate to us kids that their fathers fought in the Civil War and had sailed around the world and traveled west in a covered wagon. One lady, a prim and proper wife of a retired doctor, a Dr. Marks, retold that she was a Daughter of the American Revolution. I never met anyone that old. One gentleman regaled us with his recollection of the Battle of Belleau Wood and how the Yanks stopped the Heinnies from advancing to

Paris in 1918. He wasn't shy or sensitive when he referred to the "Frogs" as smelly and the "Limmies" as uppity. During his replay of the battle, he would drift off to sleep and I would give him a nudge in the ribs to continue. He must have climbed out of the same trench twenty times during his recollection of the battle. All in all, these stories were educational and fascinating, whether fictionalized or not.

We found many of these oldsters entertaining. Henry Kick was a ninety-plus retired printer who hailed from Brooklyn. His print shop was located just below the Brooklyn Bridge from which a sign was posted on the front window that read, "Come in. Kick the printer." Old man Henry and his sign were published in *Ripley's Believe It or Not*. Mr. Kick was also fond of telling us kids how ice cream saved his life. He was old enough to enjoy three lives and must have licked gallons of ice cream. Henry was an avid baseball fan and seldom missed any of our ball games. He also took snoozes during the day in his favorite folding chair, thus becoming a mark for many of our pranks and games. He would lay his head over the back of his chair with mouth agape. He had the nine lives of a cat, and he also had the hearing of a fifteen-year-old dog. When he dozed, we would sprinkle pebbles into his opened mouth and place his horn into his ear and shout, "Mr. Kick!" All four extremities would fly in four different directions. He would cough up the oral debris and nonchalantly respond, "Oh, it's you boys." We could have killed the old bugger. He kept licking ice cream and getting older.

I don't know who coined the phrase, but "old coots" stuck. Perhaps we found them amusing and eccentric. There was a little old lady who claimed the same red wooden bench atop the hill on the way to the Boys Cottage. As we passed her, she held a fixation at our crotches. Hence, she was dubbed the "dork lady." *Old coots* was a term of endearment. We never addressed them as such or, for that matter, by their first names. It was always and politely Mr., Mrs., or Ms. This collection of human relics was not always happy manor. Some of these codgers were downright grumpy and quarrelsome. Two such protagonists were Mr. Bauer and Mr. Bernstein.

Mr. Bauer was a slightly built man of German descent. Mr. Bernstein was a large, lantern-jawed Jew. They constantly bickered while their old-world wives sat quietly by not defending either offending spouse. We boys would take bets which one would deck the other first. Bernstein had the size, but Bauer had the quickness, albeit in slow motion. All four sat at the same dining table. They never talked and seldom passed the food dishes to one another. One would utter *"Dummkopf"* while the other would retaliate with *"Mamser!"* This verbal warfare would endure three times a day, and then a truce was declared as they shuffled off to their respective rooms where they would rehearse their next verbal strategies.

The game that I envisioned necessarily included their teeth. Each, like 99.9 percent of the old coots, wore dentures. Many of the old folks kept their dentures in a glass or Mason jar filled with a cleaning agent and placed them on the outside window ledge. As mentioned, their rooms were located on the second and third floors of Wiley Hall. This presented a challenge. How would one scale a vertical wall? Superman I was not.

The external construction and design of Wiley Hall permitted me upward mobility and access. You simply pushed your window out a full ninety degrees, climb atop the steel frames, and reach for the ledge above. You grasped the ledge and pulled yourself up to the second-floor window. While this appeared dangerous and rather ill-advised, a thirteen-year-old kid believes he is indestructible and just about immortal. Once I pinpointed Bauer's and Bernstein's rooms, I used another kid's room as my access route. Eureka! I withdrew each man's dentures from their containers and switched them.

The next morning at breakfast time, the old coots would shuffle in for their daily dose of lumpy oatmeal and cold pancakes. Of course, all the boys' eyes were on the Bauer-Bernstein table. They assumed their respective reticent positions without making eye contact with one another. Their old-world wives didn't either, waiting for the cold pancakes to be passed around the table. While each coot commanded his chair in stiff fashion, there was obvious oral movement and adjusting. Mr. Bauer's dentures were swirling around inside of Bernstein's lantern jaw, and Bernstein's choppers looked like white piano keys protruding from Bauer's hemispheric mouth. After a couple of minutes observing this odd and humorous denture fumbling, I arose and went to their table, suggesting that if each swapped their dentures, breakfast would be a much more pleasant experience. Each grudgingly obliged while muttering their Germanic-Yiddish expletives toward one another.

Of course, the boys never violated the code—a declaration of silence from each boy who may have witnessed or heard of another running afoul of the Home's rules. Frank and Mary Ellen Hall were quite amused by the theatrics and never caught on to the involvement by the boys. Pranks perpetrated on the coots were always committed outside of ear or eyeshot of anyone in charge.

One other such game was "lost in the basement." Whenever we would see one of the coots about to enter the elevator to return to their room, one of the boys would reach in and push the *B* button. Unknowingly, instead of ascending, the elevator with its unsuspecting passenger descended to the basement. The Wiley Hall basement was a catacomb of wood-making, tinsmith, electrical, printing, and plumbing shops. It also housed the music, billiards, and boxing rooms, with a few rooms for storage. In addition, it served as the entry to the indoor swimming pool.

When the elevator reached the basement, the coots would shuffle right or left, depending in which way they memorized their route to their room. Right after the *B* button was pushed, the kid would dash down the staircase and saunter toward the elevator. After a few shuffles in the supposedly correct direction, the looks of the coot would be one of bewilderment, which would give way to confusion that would culminate in wholesale fear.

The sauntering Home Kid, like Sergeant Preston, would come to the rescue and offer assistance to the lost soul. "You seem to be lost Mr./Mrs./Ms. (whomever). Can I help you?" At this moment in time, the poor coot would do anything to be escorted to his/her safe abode. Fear has a way of loosening your purse strings. The lost elderly gent or lady was safely escorted home by the hero. The "sergeant" was twenty-five cents richer.

Friday nights were movie nights at the Home. A single movie with cartoons and Movietone News were shown in the gymnasium. Nearly the entire Masonic Home community would show up for the flicks. The movie titles would be posted monthly. Errol Flynn, Burt Lancaster, and Gilbert Roland would capture our imaginations. Charles Laughton, Fred MacMurray, and William Bendix would put a sleeper hold on us. The boys wanted *Mighty Mouse*, *Heckle and Jeckle*, and *The Stratton Story*. The girls desired *Little Women*, *How Green Was My Valley*, and *By the Light of the Silvery Moon*. The old folks were content just to see the silver screen.

Most of the old folks ambled over to the gym from the infirmary, Wiley Hall, and the Vrooman Building. The folks in the hospital had to be content listening to the radio. A few had to be transported by wheelchair. This chore fell to the boys. Our assignments were permanent as permanent could be. The coots were subject to illness, had a desire to be left alone, and lived precariously with one foot on a banana peel and the other on a grave. In that case, we had the night off or were perhaps assigned to a new coot.

Wheelchair duty consisted of picking up the elderly, helping them into the chair, ignoring the odors associated with old age, wheeling them to the gym, and returning them to their rooms. Common sense dictated a modicum of safety, but not all teenagers possess the wisdom of elderly care or the common sense to avoid potential pitfalls of wheeling a wicker chair with leg supports. To us, a coot in the wheelchair was a contest in speed and daring. Some actually liked the idea of fast motion. Most were terrified.

George (or Georgie V. for short) wheeled a Mrs. Crow. She was about the size and weight of a crow but as white as a winter ptarmigan. Tommy (Yac for short) was assigned to Mrs. Benson, a woman who appeared to wearing a rucksack at all times. She was afflicted with an exophthalmic goiter and protruding eyeballs. I was the wheeler for Mr. Redfield, a very large man with a very heavy wooden leg. I swear that his leg was made from teak or mahogany. You could have made a coffee table from that leg. He was the warm-up act for the movies. He was a one-legged pipe organ player. While one leg moved rapidly to and fro thumping on the pedals, his tropical "tree" stood motionless, looking as if it were an extension of the organ.

About an hour before the movies started, we would pick up our fares. Georgie V., Yac, and George (Woodchuck for short) would walk over to the infirmary, load their passengers, and start their journeys. Roy (Roy for short) and I would hike a little farther to the Vrooman Building. Once loaded into the chairs, it was "Gentlemen, start your engines."

These kindly folks would offer us a gratuity of ten to twenty-five cents. We would turn around and wager our tips with one another. Georgie V. and Woodchuck would be the odds-on favorites because of their light loads. Yac's odds would be three to five because of that extra hump. He employed an unusual soft push so as not to jostle Mrs. Benson's rucksack. The odds for me were prohibitive because of the man and his tree. Doubling your money was incentive enough to race like hell for the gym.

The three aforementioned buildings were connected by a tunnel that traveled above ground as well as subterraneanly. Its flooring was poured concrete, with plastered interior walls and ceiling supporting the Home's heating system of steam pipes and radiators. During inclement weather, the tunnel came in handy. It was a ready-made "fast track" ideal for wheelchair drag racing. We simply advised our fares "to hold on tight." When the competition developed with full steam ahead, some of the folks would squeal a delightful "Whee" while others performed delirious wee-wees.

One evening after the movies were over, Georgie V. managed to hit a raised crack in the concrete floor of the tunnel, and poor Mrs. Crow went airborne. She crash-landed on the floor, ending up rather crumpled. Georgie offered a thousand pardons as he gathered her and gently lifted her back into her Friday-night rickshaw. Mrs. Crow continued going to the movies, but with a slower coolie at the helm.

Roy and I decided to gamble our tip money. Each of us received twenty-five cents each. It was a gamble worth taking. With Mr. Redfield's weight together with his hefty log-leg, I knew that I could take advantage of the Vrooman Building's ramps and overtake Roy. Once we got out of the slalom ramps, it was smooth sailing the rest of the way to the gym. I felt so confident of victory that I knew I could get Redfield to the gym enough to pipe another tune on the organ before Roy passed the infirmary.

Roy and I were neck and neck going down the ramps. Roy managed to slip to the inside of me, with Mr. Redfield and his piece of timber to the outside. We didn't slow down for the turns. As they say on the racing circuit, we put the pedal to the metal. As fate, or rather physics, would have it, Mr. Redfield's artificial left leg got caught in a centrifugal force, and it moved rapidly outward from the safety of his wheelchair. I felt a jerk but paid no mind. Parlaying two bits into four bits was paramount in my mind.

As Mr. Redfield yelled, "Kenny, my leg," I simultaneously caught his empty pant leg from the corner of my eye, flapping like a pennant over Yankee Stadium. "Shit, what happened? Where's his leg?" I gasped. Turning around, I saw his wooden leg jutting out from one of the cast iron radiators attached to the tunnel wall with his black shoe dangling from the stump. I gave the chair an extra push so as not to lose the momentum I had gained coming down the ramps, turned on heel, and ran back to retrieve the wayward leg. I yanked the stump from the radiator, dashed back to the propelled chair and its panicked passenger, and plopped the leg on Mr. Redfield's lap. My heroics were great; my driving was reckless. No doubt, Roy won. I lost my two bits, my pride, and damn near my job.

I wheeled into the gym a little nonplussed and prayed to the Almighty that my 'new best friend' Mr. Redfield would not spill the beans. I helped him out of the chair and onto the organ's bench, keeping the slightly scalped tree hidden from sight. Once in place, I crawled under the organ's keyboard and jerry-rigged the leg back in place. I slumped into a seat, not knowing what movie I was watching for the next hour and a half.

I returned Mr. Redfield to his room, taking the scenic route. No words were spoken. None were befitting the dramatic tunnel rally. I did not receive my twenty-five cents; nor did I receive any form of discipline. Perhaps Mr. Redfield was satisfied with the results of his test drive. I sure was impressed with that mahogany leg. It was indestructible. He was buried in two plots at the Home's cemetery: one for his torso and the other for his leg.

The Spirit of Poof

Chapel service at the Home was mandatory; no ifs, ands, or buts. Every Sunday, the congregation assembled in the Daniel D. Tompkins Memorial Chapel. The old coots came shuffling in from the Vrooman Building and Wiley Hall, jockeying for their preferred pews. Dr. William T. and Violet Clark sat in their customary pew, as did Frank and Mary Ellen Hall. Minnie Kinderwater, the nursery matron, was a no-show at times. The farm crew tended to their fields, coops, sties, and barns, preferring to evoke God's name when things went awry. Anyways, I never did see or smell any farmers in the chapel. In fact, many of the workers went elsewhere on Sundays, spending precious time with families, rolling boccie ball, or wasting away from Saturday nights.

We kids were looking angelic in our purple robes with white tunics and overflowing bow ties. In later years, the purple garments gave way to blue, the tunics remained, but the bow ties went. We looked priestly.

Chapel services were preceded by rehearsals on Thursday nights and Saturday mornings. That was the time to get the kinks out of the hymns as well as our voices. Many of the boys were experiencing puberty, and their voices made sounds like braying donkeys—like musical hee-haws. Some of us had no business singing in the chapel. It was nearly blasphemous. The head choirmaster was a taskmaster by the name of Dr. Frank Cavallo. He was a stickler for notes, pitch, and timbre. Be half an octave off, hit an F♯note rather than an Ab and he would bellow, "No, no, no. It sounds like this." He would then launch into an aria that would blow out the candles. Under all that operatic bravado was a good and kind man. He sought perfection from a bunch of tone-deaf kids. During one rehearsal, he stood next to my brother Bob to listen to the pitch. Bob monotoned the hymn "Holy, Holy, Holy." Dr. Cavallo counseled my brother not to sing. "Just move your lips, Bob."

Dr. Cavallo's music partner was Sally Blatt, the organist. Now, that lady could huff and puff those pipes. When she got cranking on that organ, the heavens opened and ten thousand angels times ten thousand angels descended upon the chapel. She could have made a million bucks if she dumped the chapel gig and went with the Jimmy Dorsey Orchestra. Sally was a loyal organist though and remained Doc Cavallo's sidekick for the remainder of my years at the Home. With their instruction, patience, and encouragement, we didn't sound half-bad. We actually created spiritual value for the old coots and nods of approval from the "Doc" and the "I."

The chapel was a New England-style house of worship. There were two rows of Tiffany stained-glass windows on each side with "Faith, Hope and Charity" prominently fixed high above and behind the pulpits. Sally's organ pipes were thrust upward, ready to fill the chapter with melodious notes. The ceiling was of stained glass, which contained the heavenly constellations. The star groupings captured my imagination during services. The rear of the chapel supported a choir loft where no choir lofted.

The chapel at the camp was of different architecture. It was built of stone and looked like an English abbey with its squared steeple. The interior was supported by heavy, rough-hewn pinewood beams and lined with pine paneling. Stained-glass windows were fixed on either side. The chapel was situated on a knoll overlooking the lake and nestled among tall pines. A stone walkway led up to the chapel, which was secured by two heavy wooden doors. The chapel was fit for an artist's palette. It was indeed a Green Cathedral.

Services were rather mundane and dreary, presided over by a Protestant minister of one faith or another. We would receive a little Baptist action, then a dull Presbyterian sermon followed by a Methodist preacher the following Sunday. The sermons lacked the hellfire and brimstone that tend to entertain the flock. The preachers talked a lot about the wonders of Jesus Christ and the great deeds he performed on innocent bystanders as well as conniving evildoers without their asking. Jesus liked to poke around in other people's business, but according to the preacher, that was okay because Jesus was the son of God. Well, I got lost in the minister's glory of Jesus and his dad and began to gaze up at the ceiling of constellations. My mind wandered about the stars with my head in a full backward tilt. When I zoomed in on Ursa Major, I felt a bearlike slap on the back of the head. It was Doc Cavallo bringing me back to Jesus and his twelve buddies. For the rest of the service, I sat glassy-eyed listening to the drone of the guy in the pulpit.

One particular minister caught our attention. I don't recall his name or rank. He was slight of physical stature, but he spoke with clarity when reading the scriptures. His diction was perfect; not a word was wasted. The reverend's sermon was as tightly structured as the walls of Jericho. He was no doubt an eighth-generation descendant of Roger Williams and educated at a prestigious Ivy League divinity school. Bernie remarked after the reverend's sermon one Sunday that he sounded like the "Spirit of Poof." I wasn't quite sure of what the "poof" meant, but it sounded right. Perhaps it was the suddenness or urgency of his ecclesiastical proverbs that punctuated his vapid sermons.

The chapel was a house for all faiths. The menorah stood next to the cross in the company of a lot of King James's Bibles, hymnals, and other trappings of Christianity. I knew there were some Jews among the old coots, and some of the boys themselves were probably born and circumcised according to the dicta of the Torah. However, rabbis were not part of the weekly program. Judaic teachings were simply absorbed by the majority of Christian doctrine. The Home gave approval for those who desired to pursue Bible study and attend Sunday school (as if Monday through Friday weren't enough) at the First Baptist Church in downtown Utica. I attended these rote-memory classes until I witnessed my brother Jim being baptized. Being dunked three times in a large fish tank was not my idea of eternal salvation. After that episode, I chose the life of a sinner.

The one memorable sermon I recall was made by Gay H. Brown, a former grand master of New York State, Supreme Court justice of New York, a Masonic icon, and a citizen who had an 11:15 am appointment with President Harry S. Truman on August 29, 1945. Mr. Brown was a barrel-chested man who ambled up the pulpit one Sunday morning, probably on St. John's Day, the holiest of Masonic days. I was waiting for one of those come-unto-Jesus sermons that would entreat me to gaze skyward at the constellations.

Gay Brown looked intently at the congregation of old coots, Masons, Eastern Star ladies, angelic kids in blue robes and white tunics, the "Doc," and the "I." He waited. Everyone was seated, waiting for wisdom to pour down from the pulpit. Somehow, Past Master Brown knew he was standing before a chapel full of charlatans.

"Some people say a nee-gar stinks! Some people call Italians wops, guineas, and greaseballs! Some people call our Jewish brothers kikes!"

The archangel Gabriel could have blown his horn and the congregation would not have heard the blast. There was silence—dead silence—throughout the chapel, including the choirless choir loft. Sally Blatt's pipes turned to cotton. I was so stunned that I couldn't recall the rest of the sermon. It didn't matter. Those three declarations were more powerful and meaningful than all the books, chapters, and verses in the Bible. I was a kid growing up among Greeks, Italians, Jews, Poles, Norwegians, Germans, Spaniards, Scots, Welsh, and French. Our names were different, but we were brothers and sisters. I felt vindicated, as did some of my brothers. Frank Hall's racism paled in comparison to Gay Brown's message of brotherly love and racial and ethnic equality.

The rest of the Sundays spiraled down to listless sermons of "do unto others." I began to gaze at the constellations again. Somewhere in those stars lay the Spirit of Poof.

St. John's Day

The Home took care of our basic needs—food, shelter, and clothing. Other amenities would be included such as free Friday-night movies, the gymnasium, playgrounds, and a summer camp. Those things and activities were greatly appreciated by us kids. As youngsters, money did not play a significant role in our lives. We simply lived off the dole. However, as we matured, there were things and activities that only money could obtain, such as baseball gloves, a personal radio, bubble gum packs that carried baseball cards, movie at a real downtown theatre, or a high school dance.

For some unknown reason, the administration did not want us to work outside the grounds, even a menial job as being a paperboy or pinsetter or mowing lawns. They never gave a reason. It was just understood with no questions asked. Perhaps they didn't want us to get too cozy with city kids or have too much social and economic independence. Whatever the reason, it was arbitrary and didn't make sense.

Being denied outside employment served only to whet our appetites for economic creativity. Pushing a wheelchair for the older folks wasn't our idea for becoming rich. Waiting for some visitor to slip you a fin wasn't going to happen either. We weren't going to steal from one another. That action was an exception to the code. If caught, you would be run through the "mill."

There were more creative avenues that led to money making. If you wanted to go to the movies, the expense would be a dollar or more. We would collect soda bottles (five cents for the small ones and twenty-five cents for the larger) and redeem them at the corner store. These coins would get us a bus ride to the downtown district. From there we would walk into the lobby of the Utica Hotel, the most fashionable lodging place, and go cushion diving into the lush chairs in order to collect loose change. With the bottle-and-cushion money, we would head straight to the movies, which would feature two movies, cartoons, Movietone News, and coming attractions, not to mention popcorn, candy, and a soda.

Our most creative endeavors were employed for the holiest of holy days in Masonic kingdom—St. John's Day. It fell on the third Thursday in June. It was a weekend affair when Masons and their wives descended upon the Home. As part of the weekend festivities, the boys and girls would stage a singing and band concert after months of practice under the tutelages of Dr. Frank

Cavallo, the choirmaster, and Lincoln Holroyd, the band director. Among Rogers and Hammerstein, Irving Berlin, and John Phillip Souza, we would bring the house down on Saturday night. On Sunday morning, the festivities took a more somber mood with the chapel filled with sweet, cherubic voices. After the proper greeting, doxology, prayer, sermon, and the final "Amen," the tours of the Home's grounds began.

Prior to the Sunday services, the boys would "spike" the indoor swimming pool located in the basement of Wiley Hall with all the coins we could muster. Of course, we were more than eager to act as tour guides for the visiting dignitaries. We would parade them by the gothic buildings, open spaces, point to the direction of the farm, and regale them with stories of scaling the water tower, playing baseball, rafting down the creek, and helping ourselves to apples in the orchard. The folks took this good-naturedly as the Masonic Home version of Tom Sawyer and Huck Finn.

Of course, the tour demanded a personal visit to the "grotto" in the basement of Wiley Hall to behold the shimmering coins that lay on the bottom of the "grotto." There were coins of every denomination. I even threw in a Canadian nickel that my grandmother had given me. (You never know. There might have been a north-of-the-border Mason in our midst.) The pump was primed. With straight faces, we acted as if the tossed coins were part of the St. John's Day tradition. Wanting to partake in this charmed tradition, the dignitaries emptied their pockets.

With the pool's bottom now a metallic pot, we concluded the tour and guided our coins-in-the-fountain tourists back to their waiting buses. Once boarded and after our fair bids of good-bye, we ran headlong to the "grotto." Like South Seas pearl divers, we dived to the bottom and collected and divvied up the loot. We were ready for the downtown movies.

A Moment of Glory

There were moments of glory in the Home. Too often the rules came into play and stifled love, creativity, and bravery. We were obliged to adhere to custom and rule the minute we entered. Independence was not a trait to pursue or admire. As children, we were to toe the line and be virtuous, thankful, and obedient. That was how the administration maintained its discipline and commonality. Woe be to the kid who sought out life carefree and unrestrained.

Bonding with one another was not as a result of therapy or child psychology. You brought your personal tragedy or sorrow with you when you were placed in the Home. Perhaps there was an older sibling to help you absorb the loss of a separation from your family. There were no group sessions with trained professionals to provide guidance through these rough and troubled times. You withdrew inward, became shy, smiled little, and spoke only when spoken to.

The first nights were lonely and frightful. You buried your head in the pillow to stifle your sobs yet wishing that someone would hear you and come to offer comfort. That didn't happen. Those in charge were too far away to hear you and too distant to care.

The boys knew who was a new Home Kid. We were curious to see him. We wanted to know your favorite baseball team, where were you from? And did you have any sisters? The new kid had suffered the same fates. The new kid would cry himself to sleep. We knew it hurt deep down inside. After a few tearful and sleepless nights, a small delegation of boys would come to visit the new kid and relate their circumstances.

"Hey, it's OK. Sammy's dad died not too long ago. Butch's mom died just last year. Roy's mom died, but his sister is living with her father" (as if to offer some hope of family reunification.) Within a week *he* became *we*. A new family was born—no parents, just kids. It was a moment of glory.

Bonding developed when the kids discovered common interests and no threat of being bullied were evident. As kids, we revered our idols, whether real or imaginary characters from the movies or comic books. There were Roy Rogers, Superman, Abbott and Costello, the Cisco Kid and Pancho, the Lone Ranger and Tonto. These heroes would live forever. Nothing could separate them from us. These were eternal friendships. They would overcome and endure any hardship.

One such friendship was between Sellars and Braddy. Like Damon and Pythias, they would be eternal friends.

Sellars's size was only matched by his strength and compassion. While not possessing a Charles Atlas physique, every fiber in his body was muscle mass. He knew it but did not flaunt it. Inside the behemoth was a profound sense of justice, a heart of gold, and the humor of a circus clown. His mission was to make for a better world. His passion was to make others laugh.

Braddy, on the other hand, was the antithesis of the big guy. He was not robust and humorous. He was diminutive and weak. He did not walk tall. He was hobbled and limped with a metal brace strapped to one leg. He was not loquacious like Sellars. Braddy's speech was mumbled and blurted. He was not strong and athletic. Brad was disabled, both mentally and physically. He was the first and only child with profound disabilities to enter the Home.

Braddy came with three siblings—sisters Paula and Donna and a fraternal twin Bruce—when he entered the Home in May 1950. Braddy was six minutes older than his six-year-old brother. He seemed to be in his own private world with his brother as caregiver. We did not know how to accept this crippled kid. He was different and weak and lacked the ability to communicate with us.

A fourteen-year old boy's sense of passion and fairness was aroused. He came out of the crowd, bent over, lifted the little one's hand, and with a gentle command, said, "Let's go for a walk, Braddy."

The pair walked away from the crowd. That moment of glory began Braddy's bonding. It was OK to cry. Sellars would be the pillow.

Of course, the administration objected to a fourteen-year-old boy acting as a therapist for a crippled kid. They were in charge, and they would care for his needs. They were too shortsighted and ignorant to recognize their own limitations, let alone Brad's. The superintendent was a general practitioner in medicine. The boys' patron was a boilermaker and his wife was perhaps a high school graduate. The matron in charge of the nursery kids was a registered nurse whose skills were honed at the turn of the century. The administration was helpless, and so was Braddy. The administration's greatest blindness was that Sellars cared.

If Sellars had a therapy plan, he kept it to himself. He was guided by his own feelings of self-worth and what was fair. His words to us were to let Braddy play with us with no special treatment, and if anyone deliberately hurt Braddy, that person would have to answer to him. These were Sellars's rules, period.

For months, the two were inseparable—holding hands, shuffling and limping to the next "therapy class." Often, Minnie Kinderwater, the turn-of-the-century nurse, would—in no uncertain terms—admonish Sellars that he was totally incapable in his assisting the crippled boy. His humor would always ward off her warnings like a horsetail shooing away a pesky barn fly. Off she would shoo in a tizzy to wait another day.

Braddy was always invited to play touch football and baseball in the backyard of Wiley Hall. Sellars made sure that Braddy got his deserved touches of the pigskin and his cuts at the plate with great cheer and applause from the "coach." Braddy would get knocked down according to Sellars's rules. Those of us who did knock him down looked over our shoulders to get the big guy's approval. Slowly but surely, the bonding among us became evident. Braddy was one of us. He was no longer different. *He* became *we*.

Sellars's next challenge was to help his charge to improve his speech, to enunciate words with clarity. Braddy's speech patterns were run-on babblings, staccato-like, making little or no sense. For hours the teacher would sit with his pupil, patiently forming words with exaggerated mouth and tongue movements. Sellars would pinch his nose, frown, and roll over backward while enunciating the word *stink*. This slapstick routine somehow made an impression on Braddy. You could see him mimicking his big brother's antics.

One day the teacher lumbered into Wiley Hall with his student in tow exclaiming, "Braddy can talk! Braddy can talk! Come on, Braddy, say icebox."

The boy wobbled to and fro and with great gusto yelled, "Aucht baucht!"

"What?" went up a chorus from the boys.

"He just said *icebox*, you guys."

Over time, the Germanic "Aucht baucht" became the Anglo *icebox*. More words rolled from Braddy's mouth.

The backyard football and baseball games continued. In the winter, Braddy was in the middle of snowball fights. He gained physical strength and self-esteem in the following years. Sellars was not through yet. He detested the metal brace that hobbled Braddy. He was determined to see the day when Braddy would rid himself of this cruel reminder of being a child with a physical handicap. He dared to remove the brace, and for days on end, Sellars would administer physical therapy to Braddy's leg. He encouraged him how to place one foot in front of the other while grasping his arms and legs. The encouragement never ceased.

"All right, Braddy, you can do it. Come on, one foot at a time. Good Braddy."

One day the brace was gone. No one said a word, especially the administration. They were chagrined. Braddy was proud. St. Sellars contemplated his next "miracle." Braddy no longer shuffled. He put one foot in front of the other just like his big brother said. It was a moment of glory.

Butch

Butch was one of the original nursery nine when I entered the Home in 1944. He and his brother, George, arrived a month before the Pettit four. He wasn't quite seven when I arrived, but he was a big seven. Butch was one of those 'tweeners—too big for the nursery, but too young for Wiley Hall, where the middle-sized and big boys resided. For the sake of survival, the administration placed him in the nursery for the time being. Butch would have held his own with the older boys had he been placed in Wiley Hall.

The Sellars boys hailed from Washington Heights in the upper Manhattan neighborhoods of New York City. He came to the Home with the nickname of "Butch." His given name was James, about as Scottish as a lad could be. As Butch matured, I always pictured him and his brother walking the streets of New York City. George probably had his little brother on a leash and dared any neighborhood kid to pet his sibling, saying, "Don't mess with Butch. He won't growl, but he'll bite you. He's a Scottish bulldog!"

Their father, John, emigrated from Scotland, probably fearing that any future sons would devour all the sheep from the

Highlands and maybe a pony or two. God, those boys were big and strong as oxen. Butch simply outgrew the nursery and no doubt was sick and tired of Miss Manna's daily bowel-movement demands. I imagined Butch returning to his father's land and becoming one of those British marines.

He was like a block of granite—rough and solid. He wasn't as big as his older brother. He didn't have to. He was tough and he knew it, but he held back his aggressions until the game started. He was ultimately fair, but he didn't hold back. Doggone, he looked like what a guy named Butch should look like except for the hairdo. He was missing the crew cut, but that was not his doing. The Home's administration frowned on such shoddy looks.

As Butch grew, so did his prowess for sports. He was big, strong, and somewhat agile for a boy his size. In high school, he was a four-letter sport athlete. He excelled in baseball, football, track, and basketball. Eventually, he was selected as a collegiate All-American football player. He was probably the best athlete that came from the Home, which produced more than its share of athletes. When playing either with or against Butch, you mastered the art of giving him ample clearance. When he walked in a crowd, he would bow his head, not make eye contact, and lo and behold, he parted the Red Sea. People gave way or they would end up on the sidelines. He was a human bulldozer.

All of us had roommates in our teens. Usually you were paired by age and size and, oddly, not by bloodlines. For some inexplicable reason, the administration seemed hell-bent on keeping blood brothers apart. It didn't occur to them to maintain the last vestiges of family among kids. It was part of the "plan of separation" for Home Kids. Forget your past, dress alike, and obey the rules. They did this with such seeming ease without regard to familial feelings.

Butch's roommate was Tom. It was one of those marriages made in heaven. Butch was Tom's foil, his test animal. Tom's favorite pastime, other than art, was playing dumb like a fox. Tom would advertise, and Butch would take the bait, much to Tom's glee. When Butch would protest, Tom would demur, "Who, what, when, me, wait Butch, not me."

And I'll be damned if Butch wasn't outsmarted for the umpteenth time. Tom was clever enough not to bring ridicule upon Butch. That could have proven fatal.

Once when Butch was asleep—dead-to-the-world kind of sleep—Tom placed a vial of some god-awful smelling stuff under Butch's nose. It would have gagged a maggot. Not Butch—he continued his Rip van Winkle slumber right through the stench with all of us in attendance. When Butch awoke, not a peep was made with the exception of the roomie, who inquired of Butch if he experienced a bad dream. Whether the response was in the affirmative or the negative, Butch fell for the bait. He spent the next several hours asking Tom why he asked such a question. Tommy never let on or made a slip of the tongue or those in attendance.

Tom had a reputation of stinking up the place with his overactive gastrointestinal blasts. He could "float a vapor biscuit" that would clear out a chicken ranch. Tom ate the same stuff we ate, but the guy had a supercharged boiler for a stomach. In fact, he had his own bathroom that none of us dared to enter. Butch was simply the victim of Tom's foul habits. Down the hallway of Wiley Hall, you would hear Butch's plaintive cries, "Geez, Tom, not again!"

"What . . . who . . . me . . . naw, Butch. You're smelling the cleaning fluid they pour on the floor."

He did it again, and Butch fell for the diversion.

Once, Butch challenged Tom's alibi by pointing out the brown stain on their dormitory wall.

"See, right there, Tom. That's your fartin' wall."

Tom couldn't escape that time. He boasted of his accomplishment of backing up to the wall, dropping his trousers, and letting go with a stupendous fart. Over time, the wall was as colored as Da Vinci's *Last Supper*.

Butch accepted Tom as a top-notch roommate. They were good balance. Butch was rough-hewn while Tom was smooth. Butch liked T-shirts; Tom preferred Mr. B collars. Butch was the athlete while Tom was the artist.

Like his older brother, Butch was ultimately fair. He played by the rules and expected the same from you. If you played dirty or used unnecessary foul language, Butch was ready and willing to invoke the rules. In a game of touch football in the backyard of Wiley Hall, one of the boys, Larry, got very aggressive and unsportsmanlike with a "whip block" on one of the younger kids. Butch was incensed and challenged Larry. The latter made one of the biggest mistakes of his life and accepted the challenge. Larry was older than Butch but not bigger. There wasn't much fighting among the boys, but this one was a doozy. It was one-sided from the beginning, with Butch pummeling Larry at will. Larry wouldn't give in or cry uncle. Sellars stepped in and pulled his little brother off the bleeding Larry.

I too felt Butch's sense of justice one summer at the camp. He was the appointed counselor for the boys. My first counselor was Ed "Clunk" Wallace. My last one was Jim "Butch" Sellars. How's that for masculinity. It was the practice of dividing up the kids into teams to engage in various sports and activities. We were playing a form of soccer with my team on a rather embarrassing losing end. The game ended, and all I could think of was going for swims in the lake. Butch declared that we had more time to play another game. Out of frustration of yet another one-sided loss, I muttered, "Shit."

Butch said, "Come over here, Kenny."

I walked over to where he and Mary, the girls' camp counselor, were standing, and Butch said, "What did you just say?"

"Shi—"

Never did finish the word. *Pow!* Butch punched me flush on the jaw. I saw stars, but for some reason, I didn't hit the deck.

Mary was shocked and in a surprised expression asked, "Buuutch?"

I had it coming, no two ways about it. I ran afoul of Butch's fairness doctrine and made an ass out of myself. Later, we discussed the incident, and I understood his rules. He never apologized. He didn't have to. It was my fault. I liked Butch better after that day. He may have been a ready-fire-aim guy, but he was one of the fairest kids at the Home.

George and Johnny

Brothers argue. By their nature, they seek to be the stronger, the wiser, become the leader or lover. They seek the family's attention and favoritism. They compete with one another and play hard. Georgie V. and Johnny V. never engaged in fraternal competition. They complemented one another. They were constellations.

George and John came to the Home in 1943, a year prior to my admittance. The brothers were of Greek origin with swarthy complexions and black hair. Georgie, the older brother, was dramatic and engaging. Johnny was introspective and reserved. The older was stocky; the younger was chiseled. Johnny was the first Home Kid that I encountered. We quickly became "brothers," as did all the boys in our years together at the Home. Georgie was ten months older than me, and Johnny was six months younger. During my thirteen years at the Home, I never slept more than twenty feet from either one.

Our years in the nursery were spent playing with the other kids and mollifying Miss Manna's demands for daily bowel movements. Other than that horrible time spent in the nursery's coal cellar and the trek to Wiley Hall, we progressed in natural order. That is, we were generally the same in clothing, manners, and punctuality. We seldom socialized with the big kids residing in Wiley Hall or the Knights Templar Building, with the exception of an occasional visit from my older natural brothers. We were somber, disciplined, and altogether shy. There were no parental figures to instill confidences, social skills, or self-worth. We made do with what we had—ourselves.

Sometime during the latter half of the '40s we migrated to Wiley Hall to take up residence on the first floor. The upper two floors were occupied by the big kids, and under no circumstances were we permitted to travel up the stairwells. Who would want to? We were simply too frightened to dare such a foolish attempt. The restriction to the first floor did not grant us immunity from the whims of the older boys. Those who did not bail out of their second- and third-floor dormitory windows or use the back stairwells traversed through the hallway of the first floor.

There was a definite pecking order among the boys. We little guys gave way to the big guys as they sauntered through or else you were subject to a "scoff," which was an open-handed, upward slap on the back of the head. We looked like prairie dogs, bobbing our heads in and out of our dorm rooms, when the big guys cruised by. This might-makes-right environment greatly influenced our maturation. Some of us would replicate that behavior as we matured while others found a more humane and sensible pattern of behavior. George and Johnny sought the more sensible pattern.

The brothers were always on their best behaviors, never sassy, charitable, and honest to a fault. They were the most popular brothers when they received a package of the famous "sandwich cookies" from their grandparents; the boys would queue up when the package arrived, knowing that the contents were the most delicious treat ever tasted. Rather than hoarding this honeyed bounty, the boys graciously parceled out the *baklava!* Georgie V., as he came to be called, was more of the extrovert. He was engaging, dramatic, and demonstrative—not bellicose but not shy. Johnny, on the other hand, was the introvert. He was introspective, even-tempered, and controlled—not sullen or moody. Each was studious and achieved honor-roll status in their educational pursuits. Georgie verbalized his status while Johnny internalized his role. Each found peace in their stylized lives. Their sole acts of aggression were limited to a pinecone war and the Coke-bottle affair. I happened to be involved in both skirmishes—the latter, much to my pain and suffering.

During the summer, the brothers' paternal and maternal grandparents would visit them at the camp, spending a week at the cottages located in Woodgate. Each day, the entourage would trek the three miles to the camp and return to their one-room cottages by nightfall, politely declining free car rides by Marv Allen, the camp's caretaker. Their clothing was odd. They dressed in black suits and black ankle-length dresses. There was mysticism about their attire—foreign and very black. They conversed in hushed tones in their Hellenic language. The boys seemed to comprehend the words, but to the rest of us, *it was all Greek.* The grandparents enjoyed the lake and its perimeter trail. They would take long strolls, and upon returning, they would wade into the shallows, enjoying the cool water as if it flowed down from Mt. Olympus. Although looking and speaking old-world, they seemed to enjoy us *Amerikanos.*

It was during the summer months when the brothers playacted their acts of "aggression." Three of us were tossing pinecones about when we consciously made the decision to toss them at each other. Like most acts of aggression, things became escalated. The initial tosses were mature pinecones—the brown ones—lightweight with open husks. When it became obvious that these oldies had an uncertain flight path, the immature green cones were employed in our game of "dodge cone." These natural projectiles, when thrown, had a more reliable flight path. Mistakenly, Johnny picked up a rock and threw it at his brother, hitting him directly in the eye and sending Georgie to the nearby infirmary. It was a serious, but not a permanent injury. For the rest of the summer, Georgie wore sunglasses, looking like the famous Clark Gable.

The other act of "hostility" involved Georgie and me. It occurred not too far from the pinecone-war site. One early evening, prior to the Friday-night movies, the kids were at the candy store where ice cream, candy, and sodas were sold and dispensed. Outside of the store, I grabbed Georgie's Coke bottle and vigorously shook it to the point where the soda erupted from the bottle. To say the least, Georgie was incredulous, but he didn't know quite what to do.

Rudy, an older kid and somewhat on the sadistic side, caught Georgie's eye and gave him the thumbs-down signal with a nod of the head. Georgie took this as a sign of approval from an older kid that "might makes right" and reclaimed his bottle and thereupon proceeded to conk me on the head. Needless to say, I saw stars and was covered in blood. I never grabbed a soda bottle from someone else's grasp again, and I despised Rudy's "Nero" role-playing. Georgie apologized, and we got back to the business of being brothers again.

To say that Georgie was dramatic was an understatement. His attire was impeccable, his wavy black hair neatly combed, and his speech patterns possessed a flair. He was an excitable guy with a bundle of energy to light up the stage. He could also whack a pretty good fastball, thus earning an additional nickname, "Joe D.," after the great Joe DiMaggio.

His excitability manifested itself one evening on Round Lake. When returning from a fishing expedition, Georgie was relaxing at the stern of a boat while one of the other kids handled the oars. For some inexplicable reason, Georgie was twirling split-shot sinkers between the forefingers and thumbs of each hand against his ears. The lake's waters were calm, no threats of explosive mines existed, and no dive-bombers were in the air. Somehow one of the sinkers slipped and rolled into an ear. This miscue overactivated his nerve center, and in reaction to this faux pas, the remaining sinker slipped from Georgie's fingertip grasp and rolled into the other ear.

Immediately, Georgie leaped up. "I can't hear! I can't hear!" he excitedly exclaimed.

The oar-bearer, who hadn't seen the avalanche of lead roll into Georgie's ears, was puzzled. "What?"

"I can't hear, I can't hear!" Georgie repeated in disbelief of his miscues but convinced that he would face a life of permanent deafness. In an attempt to dislodge the sinkers, Georgie jammed his fingers into his ears, serving only to exacerbate the situation.

This "Can't hear! What?" drama continued across the lake, into the boat dock, past the rock garden, and up to the boys' cottage. Once inside the cottage, Georgie had to loudly proclaim to each of us that he couldn't hear and that deafness was imminent. Of course, these bursts of Greek tragedy played well with his audience. We recognized Georgie's penchant for drama and responded in kind. We began to lip-synch without the audio. We formed words without sound. Georgie was convinced beyond all hope that he was indeed doomed to a world of eternal silence. The clincher was when big George grabbed the deaf George by the ankles and shook him upside down. The sinkers defied gravity and clung to the earwax. Georgie spent the rest of the night mumbling, "I can't hear . . . I can't hear . . . I can't . . . I . . ."

The next morning, a "miracle" occurred at the local hospital.

Georgie V. was also the victim to poison ivy and a near victim to an icy drowning, both disasters occurring at Starch Factory Creek. He was one of those people who had no immunity against poison ivy/oak or sumac. He would simply hear the word and he would immediately break out into a class A rash over 99 percent of his body. We used to engage in war games down in the creek, which was a heavily wooded area with loads of brambles and poison ivy. Well, Georgie caught the rash and ended up in the hospital. As the nurse was applying a lotion on his body, including his private parts, Georgie's "unit" began to rise and stiffen. Why not, he was a teenager whose testosterone was beginning to rage. The attending nurse, who must have received her medical training at a Gurkha training camp, gave one backslap that crumpled his penile rod. We never let Georgie forget the horror of that incident. Georgie never let us forget that the cure was worse than the disease.

Starch Factory Creek almost claimed Georgie during one winter afternoon. We would ice-skate on the frozen creek from the Home downstream to the falls at Proctor Park, about a mile's distance. You had to watch for boulders that protruded through the frozen ice and holes or weak ice. Georgie went through the ice, and the current carried him downstream. Our fear, and his, was that he would get caught at the lip of the falls and drown. Those of us fortunate to be still on the ice skated downstream, looking for an opening. We could see Georgie frantically peering upward through the ice in mortal fear. Luckily, we found an opening in the ice prior to the falls and were able to drag the frenetic "otter" out of the water. His clothing immediately froze to the point where he could not bend at the joints. We carried Georgie home like a Yule log and dumped him into a bathtub to thaw.

If drama was Georgie's stage, then solemnity was Johnny's space. The younger brother was bookish, observant, and sensitive. Johnny revered all things living, whether animal, plant, or spirit. He never disturbed their space or being. He sought peace and eschewed conflict. His spirit was indomitable. Not only was his spirit steadfast, but Johnny possessed the ability to block out pain. It was as if he separated pain from injury. One was to endure, and the other to experience. At times, his being was more spiritual than mortal.

As young boys of about eight years, Johnny and I were playing in the backyard of Wiley Hall. Malcolm, a brutish sixteen-year-old, approached us with bow and arrow in hand. Malcolm was called Ape by the older boys mainly because of his mind and muscle. He sought attention through machismo, which roughly translated into being stupid. Malcolm told Johnny to stand still so that he would shoot an arrow close by like William Tell of old. Malcolm missed, but Ape hit his target. The arrow pierced into Johnny's thigh. Ape loped for the trees while Johnny pulled the arrow out. I believe that Johnny was more shocked by the mindless act than the sting of the arrow. This was not the sport of kings.

Johnny was not into sports like the rest of us. Many of the boys collected baseball cards and read the sports pages. Johnny collected nature's wonders and read poetry and novels. We were challenged by fastballs; he was challenged by Tennyson. Not that Johnny was timid or uncoordinated; he was more Athenian than Spartan. He was bored by sports yet possessed great athleticism himself. Once, during our high school years, Johnny was waiting for me for me to finish my practices on the track team, and the coach attempted to enlist him for the team. Johnny's response was the usual "Naw, don't want to." The coach kept harping until Johnny relented and took off running down the long-jump runway. He leaped farther than the team's ace long jumper, clad in his street clothes and barefoot. The coach was aghast, and Johnny simply shrugged, "Let's go home, Kenny."

We walked home not discussing his cinderman heroics.

My Greek brother was not a loner. He engaged the surroundings on his terms—social but not "showing his hand." He would contemplate his next move without fanfare or flourish. Johnny would glide effortlessly into the next scene. Perhaps that was the basis for his nickname, "Beaver."

The brothers were a constellation. Like Castor and Pollux, they were the brightest stars in the Gemini heavens as well as in the Home.

Swede

Richard entered the Home in the early '50s. He hailed from the mean streets of New York. Though not combative, he would proudly display his scar as a result of his skirmishes. Richard's toughness was softened when his sister, Sonja, referred to her older brother as Richie. The boys saw him otherwise.

"Swede" was Nordic with a nose that looked like an avalanche cascading from his forehead. He had a cocked eye and a shock of thick hair that took root in his head. He gave the appearance of the mythical Thor. This Nordic thought nothing of the chilly waters of Round Lake, which was spring fed. While most of the kids would retreat to their towels and bathrobes, Swede would romp and breach the waters like a carefree seal. No water was too cold.

While not a twinkle toes, Swede could hold his own when it came to sports. He was a block of granite. While engaged in a softball game at the camp, Swede blocked the plate when Bruce slid in. You guessed it, *crack!* Bruce's femur broke like a pretzel. The granite never shattered. That horrific break broke up our card game of pitch. We had a foursome of Swede, Bernie,

Bruce, and me. For hours we played endless pitch, keeping score to see which loser would have to treat the winner with an ice cream or soda pop. The broken leg never deterred us. Bruce was ambulanced to the hospital in Utica, but the game continued. It was decided that we would use the daily supply-truck run as the conveyor of bids and cards. Bernie opined that this makeshift bridging was unworkable. He exclaimed, "It'll be Christmas before a hand is played!"

Everyone folded their cards.

We Did the Time Within the Crime

The Masonic Home had an abundance of two adventure places—old redbrick buildings and the real estate they were situated on. The land was created by the cataclysmic forces of nature, and the buildings were created by the charitable forces of man. As boys growing up in a strict by-the-rules environment, these adventure places would recede when we attempted to explore them or whose curios were always out of reach when we tried to touch them. To be successful, one had to be brazen, possess a disdain for the rules, be dumb as a doorknob, and religiously adhere to the code. The code was passed down like ritual from the prior generation of orphans. Simply stated: *Do not rat on a Home Kid!*

The real estate, which was 1,600 acres, encompassed more than a dozen buildings, a farm with barns, coops, sties, a creamery, two residences, an apple orchard, corn and wheat fields. The Home was a virtual city within a city with its own autonomous government, much like the Vatican within the Eternal City. Many of these buildings were connected by a tunnel that ran above and below ground level. In addition, the place had its expansive lawns, a baseball field, hills, a cemetery, and a creek coursing through the wooded areas. Tom Sawyer and Huck Finn would have whitewashed the Great Wall of China to have had access to this Mohawk Valley paradise.

It was the buildings that drew our attention. Built in the first quarter of the twentieth century, these redbrick Gothic structures were museums dedicated to memories of the rich and famous within the Masonic community and filled with idle treasures. Each was adorned with a cornerstone and chiseled with the name of an American Mason. The chapel was dedicated to the memory of Daniel D. Tompkins, James Monroe's vice president; Robert R. Livingston, the diplomat who negotiated the Louisiana Purchase and administered the oath of office to our first president George Washington, was engraved on the library and museum; Wiley Hall was selected as the edifice to William J. "Pop" Wiley, who served as the Home's superintendent from 1906 to 1945; the memorial building was constructed with the financial assistance from the famous actor, Edwin Booth; and the Soldiers and Sailors Memorial Hospital was erected as a memorial to all the Masons who gave their lives during World War I. Additionally, to throw into the Masonic mix was the construction of the Knights Templar (KT) Building, which served as the older girls' residence. The Knights were the gentlemen who donned the chapeau, a naval hat with the feathery plume who raised engraved swords. But it was the Charles Smith Infirmary that got our attention as an adventure place.

The infirmary was constructed in 1907 as a hospital for the care of residents. The Soldiers and Sailors Memorial Hospital was subsequently constructed, and the infirmary became a residence building for seniors, with the ground floor carved into separate rooms for storage. This building was situated in the center of the Home's campus and served as a Trojan horse. The tunnel ran in each direction to and from the ground floor. Across from the tunnel was another room that served as living quarters for George Kean, the disgruntled Wiley Hall dishwasher who spent most of his time talking with himself over cheap wages, lack of respect given by the head cook, Home Kids, and anyone else within his self-audible/verbal range. George possessed another strange anomaly, a physical one. He had a significant indentation in the right temporal bone of his head. It looked like he took a ricocheted musket ball off his noggin. I was told by the head cook, Bert Berrus, that old George got bitten by a dog. Maybe that's why George griped about his boss. Being bitten in the head by a dog was tragic.

Between the infirmary and the administration building were the paint shop and more storage rooms tied together by yet another tunnel. In short, the infirmary ground-floor storage rooms were in the eye of the storm, ready for accepting the Trojan horse. This was an adventure place with an abundance of booty.

The aforementioned code assumed that silence was golden because the older Home Kids had scouted out the infirmary and were biding their time to roll in the "horse." No younger kid would dare to prematurely jump out of the starting gate. If one committed that error in judgment, he would pay the consequences of the Black Hand or pass through the "mill." The Black Legion consisted of an inner secret society of older boys who would not hesitate to commit holy terror. I never witnessed or heard any demonizing, witchcraft, or bloodletting, so I believed the Black Hand to be a very effective myth. The "mill," however, was very real, very punishing, and was administered with the approval of the boys' patron. The guilty party was forced to crawl on all fours between the legs of all (preferably older) boys who applied wooden paddles, belts, and rolled magazines to the backside of the guilty. Some of the bullies would clamp their knees against your body, thus immobilizing you for additional and unwarranted paddling. Justice was swift with little or no chance of appeal or revenge. The code did not permit or entertain democracy.

The administration of the Home was a top-down style of command and control. All authority was vested with the superintendent who assiduously parceled out lesser roles of authority to his minions who were identified with the misnomers of *matrons* and *patrons*. These guardians were not the Father Flanagans or Florence Nightingales graciously tending to the emotional needs of children. To the contrary, they were the messengers, the martinets, and the servile flatterers. Their sole source of authority was to seek transformation from their human larvae to that of an adult praying mantis readying to grasp their youthful prey. That morphing was fostered and often rewarded. It kept the kids dependent and awarded the martinets with an executive dining room.

My older brother Jim somehow learned about the infirmary storage rooms, probably from his older brothers. Sometimes blood does run thicker than water, and it sure did ignore the code. After much cajoling and threats of ratting, my brother relented and took myself and a few of my contemporaries on a scouting mission into the bowels of the infirmary. The mission was a look-see, confirmation of the existence of the booty, and a hastened exit. My brother was not brazen, adhered to the rules, and feared the code.

I was impudent, ignored rules, but honored the code.

The brief mission served to heighten my curiosity and created my desire to loot and become the renegade rule-breaker. Willie Sutton answered the question of why he robbed banks—because that's where the money is. I was going into the infirmary because that's where the adventure was.

My fourteen-year-old mind began to plan. The plan was simple. Just get a bunch of guys. The joint was in the eye of the storm. We don't need anyone to play scout. It was early spring; snow was still on the ground, hence, no baseball. Let's sneak in on a Saturday afternoon. We'll be protected by the brick walls, the old coots won't hear us, the administration building is closed, George Kean will be talking up a blue streak, and the tunnels will serve as our exit. Great plan!

It was Saturday. The time was now. Roy, Wayne, and Johnny were the only enlistees. The others obeyed the rules and feared the code. Their declination to join was a guarantee of silence, win or lose.

The storage rooms were guarded by a steel-grated wall that went from the floor to two feet shy of the ceiling. A hinged door, centered in the wall, of the same design and construction was locked. No skeleton key would work. It was altogether a different lock. We had to scramble up the grated wall, shimmy through a two-foot opening and slide down the other side. We were in.

Once inside, it was an eenie-meenie-minee-moe proposition. No one sanctum was more valuable than the other. There was no precedence or priority. It was a free-for-all pillage into steamer trunks teeming with clothing, costume jewelry, coins, corsets, high-heeled shoes, neckties, postage stamps, knives, pocket watches, black-and-white family photographs, and just plain schlock. These were the personal items of Masonic Home residents who passed away and left no living relatives. The administration stored these belongings into trunks for eternity or for the eternally vigilant praying mantis. Our thoughts were why should *they* plunder the loot when it was here for *our* pickings?

It was a no-brainer to eliminate the *they* from the pillaging equation. All hell broke loose! For two hours, the hole-in-the-steel-grate gang rifled through trunks with reckless abandon. Clothes, high heels, and photographs were flying. Occasionally, one of us would squeeze into a corset, wear the costume jewelry, and ogle the coins. Enthusiastically, we tossed containers of talcum powder, facial makeup like the kind your grandmother applied in ample amounts, as well as granulated soaps and mothballs. Of course, Sir Isaac Newton was right. Gravity was and is a great influence. Everything hit the floor simultaneously with a composition of snow on snow. With our looting satiated, we reversed our course. We also left a trail like snowshoed fur trappers.

We scrambled up the grated wall, shimmied through the opening, and slid down the other side. Our pockets were bulging with treasure and schlock. We made our exit through the tunnel by twos. Roy and Wayne walked easterly while Johnny and I hightailed in the opposite direction. By separating, we were convinced that we would look invisible yet seen. By separation, silence commenced. Forever after, the code would be invoked.

A week passed. The code still had its silver lining, and silence was glittery gold.

Into the following week, the message was delivered. This is one time I would not have hesitated to shoot the messenger. Whenever matters of high concern arose, the boys were directed to assemble in the Wiley Hall library. The messenger: Frank Hall. He was uniquely and totally unqualified to supervise, nurture, or discipline anyone under the age of forty, let alone teenagers. His sole qualification was that he was a supreme sycophant who happened to be a Mason. His conversations were dull sermons laced with fabrications. He had the vision of a dog—black-and-white. He was a racist and a boilermaker. His wife, Mary Ellen, was kinder. Two questions: Who the hell hired him? Why?

The sermon invariably started with "The Doc and I . . ." This time the "Doc" got wind that a break-in had occurred in the Smith Infirmary, and by god, he was going to get to the bottom of this. Without a blink or hesitation, the code began to swarm into the library. There were no "gee whizzes," "huhs," or "I'll be darneds" uttered. Silence commanded, and in no way was there a notion of retreat.

Suddenly, silence was fractured. The code was on a precipice. Bernie yelled, "City kids!" According to accepted tradition, the world was divided between Home Kids and city kids. Home Kids were us. We represented goodness, virtue, and truth. City kids were those boys who resided outside the Home. They were outsiders, mainly from East Utica, and primarily Italian. They represented roughness, Catholicism, and greasy salami. They were not to be trusted under any circumstance. The administration's xenophobia played into the Home Kids' hands. We went to high school with city kids, played on the same teams, and danced with their sisters. In a twisted sense, they were our foils. When the heat was about to scorch and alibis nonexistent, you declared, in self-defense, "City kids." 99.9 percent of the time, the city-kid defense exonerated us.

This time, the defense faltered. The "Doc" and "I" had done their homework. Like French inspectors, the duo deduced that we were guilty, that city kids didn't have a clue where the infirmary was, let alone what was stashed in its bowels, and that George Kean never mentioned their presence while mumbling. The coup de grâce was the powder on the floor at the scene of the crime.

Before the "Doc and I" meeting ever started, our Red Ball high-top sneakers were ferreted out and matched with the imprints laid in grandmother's makeup. Only two prints were identified. The others were obscured in the joy of looting. Johnny and I were nabbed by our snowshoe trail. The evidence was incontrovertible. We were caught. No city kids this time. The code was still intact, but the silence was a bit tarnished.

Of course, there was no appeal process. Punishment was to be swift and harsh. There would be no convocation of the mythical Black Hand. The "mill" was dismantled. Punishment would be administered by Rudy, a Home Kid with Machiavellian principles. Rudy had been a Home Kid since 1934 and spent a career at the Home, interrupted by the army and college. He was musically, artistically, and athletically talented. He was also cruel and predacious. In any event and much to Rudy's delight, the "Doc" directed the "I" to see that punishment was to be executed.

Johnny and I accepted the decision without violating the code. For self-survival, a plan was concocted whereby scarves would be inserted into our pants' bottoms to absorb the strikes of the wooden paddle. Once contact was made, the one who was summonsed first would let out a wail. We were led to the basement of Wiley Hall to await our fate. Two weeks ago, we were in one basement filled with felonious glee, and now we are in another basement in stunned fear.

Lots were drawn, and Johnny was first up. He shuffled his way into a closed-door room, fearing for his life and fearing that the scarf would slip off his buttocks. *Whack!* Nothing. *Whack!* Nothing. A long pause ensued. *Whack!* One hell of a wail erupted from the room. My thoughts, from the other side of the wall, were *Attaboy, Johnny, great acting.* Johnny emerged from closed doors with the most pained expression, tears running down his cheeks, heaving with such sobs that his ribs were exposed like a prisoner of war. My thoughts continued, *Beautiful, Johnny, you're better than the movies.*

I was next. The "executioner" was poised with paddle raised. The "I" commanded that I assume the "angle." I waited for that first whack, wondering if I could match Johnny's thespian heroics. The "I" then commanded that I remove the scarf from my pants.

The "Doc," the "I," and the Executioner were bastards!

Phase 1 of punishment was completed. Johnny and I couldn't sit for days. The Predator preened, the "I" acted like nothing happened, and I could care less about the "Doc." Phase 2 was ball-and-chain imprisonment. The judgment rendered was 24/7 confinement to Wiley Hall, excepting for school attendance and chapel service. Every Saturday (all of Saturday) we were to sweep, mop, clean, scrub, wash, sanitize, and dust every square inch of the bowels of the infirmary for the next three months! To a couple of fourteen-year-old boys, this was tantamount to a life sentence.

Common law determined our guilt, but the laws of creativity would lighten the ball and chain. Armed with slop buckets, brooms, mops, rags, brushes, gallons of witch hazel, and a wheelbarrow full of Spic and Span, Johnny and I went about our business as junior Tonys. It took us the full day to clean up the mess of corsets, photographs, high heels, grandmother's powder, and the schlock. Guess what? We had fourteen Saturdays left.

When a fourteen-year-old kid has fourteen Saturdays left after the work is done, it's highly unlikely that he's going to volunteer to wash out a birdbath. The Law of Creativity was enacted. Back to the steamer trunks and open sesame. Undo all the laces in the corsets and the high-heeled shoes. Tie them together into a great ball of twine. Tie one end to the center steel-grated door, continue to run the laces alongside of the water pipes attached to the ceiling, and tie the other end to an upright broom handle. For test purposes, open the steel-grated door. Yep, the broom was yanked to the floor. Beta test was a success.

Now that the security system was in place, time for creativity was nigh. We strategically placed water-filled slop buckets in all rooms, mops were ready for wringing, brooms were set in place, with witch hazel and Spic and Span ready for the pour. For entertainment we smuggled in Chinese checkers and a deck of cards. We facetiously contemplated posting a "Welcome, Come on In" sign at the gate. We didn't. Before he could make three unannounced steps, Frank Hall caused the broom to fall, which sounded a call to general quarters.

Phase 3 was the stunner. With the "I" at bay and the "Doc" receiving favorable reports concerning our ball-and-chain confinement, Johnny and me looked at one another and, in unison, said, "Let's complete the job." For the next six Saturdays, we methodically and meticulously searched and looted every single steamer trunk. We smuggled out that which we believed was of value or worth trading and left the schlock for the praying mantis. The contents of those trunks were left in a neater state than when initially stored.

Phase 4 was the icing on the cake. By a stroke of luck, Johnny's father, Silas, a gregarious Greek, was coming to visit his two sons, George and Johnny, and would arrive at the Home next Friday. The administration was apoplectic. No dues-paying, lodge-attending Mason was going to visit his sons when one was chained to a slop bucket. Good old Silas got his Greek son and his French Canadian brother a pardon. God bless the Greeks!

To the "Doc," the "I," and the Executioner—too bad. The code was left unscathed, and silence regained its brilliant luster. We did the time within the crime.

Franklin Kenneth Hall

Frank Hall was a curious guy. He was appointed as the boys' patron in 1946. Prior to his appointment, he was a boilermaker in the Home's heating factory, a place where coal was shoveled into huge furnaces that heated most of the buildings through a series of pipes running through a tunnel that connected six multistoried buildings. Now, that's a leap!

He hailed from Syracuse, New York, was an identical twin, achieved a high school education, married his childhood sweetheart, Mary Ellen, and together had a daughter. You would think that as a turn-of-the-century guy, he reached his pinnacle. Not so. He had to show his talents in child psychology by leading a batch of multiethnic, somewhat dysfunctional, and love-starved boys. In short, his work was cut out for him.

In order to overcome his shortcomings, Frank resorted to his basic instincts of carpentry, bigotry, and wannabe-outdoorsman. He performed well with the first instinct, excelled at the second, and failed miserably with the third. He built speedboats from plywood and erected a "River Kwai" bridge over the camp's trout stream. On the Friday-night Gillette boxing matches, he longed to see the "dirty wop" and the "nigger" get pummeled.

He was at a total loss if the two pugilists squared off in the ring. His outdoorsmanship consisted of an irrelevant ding-dong rock bass and make-believe stories of his hunting prowess.

Somehow, one of the boys hung a moniker on Frank. It was Fritz. It was a good name. It described him well—like huh? The name was invoked as a code word when the boys spoke disparagingly of Frank. When Frank marched between the bunks at the boys' cottage, wearing his Fruit of the Loom underwear and sneezing "Brusha," the boys would relay the code, "Here comes Fritz."

Frank had two hobbies. One was buying a Hudson automobile every two years. He said a Hornet was better than a Wasp. Hell, we didn't know the difference between a bee and an anteater. And we didn't care much either. His other hobby was that of an animal lover. He owned a Scottish terrier by the name of Skippy and a parakeet by the name of Silver. One of the boys "accidentally" left the window open, and poor Silver bit the proverbial silver bullet and flew to bird heaven. Over the years, age got the better of Skippy. He began to collect warts and sores and he turned blind and bumped into all kinds of things. Mrs. Hall evened accused the boys of deliberately placing obstacles in Skippy's way. Skippy's antagonist was a duck. That beaked bird would peck poor Skippy's ass, much to the delight of the boys and to the dismay of the Halls. One night, *pop*. The Halls had roasted duck in their private dining room.

Perhaps the weirdest habit of Frank Hall was his misguided medical approach to any malady. He would purposely bleed his fingertips with a razor to rid himself of the poisons that invaded his body. The last guy to undergo that procedure was George Washington! Fritz's spatulate fingers were worthy of such a medical procedure. May he rest in peace.

The Doc and I

"The Doc and I" was a phrase oft repeated by Frank Hall. In his own mind, the phrase gave him stature in the administration's pecking order. It was the deliberate isolation of the boys from the center of authority in order to cause a rift that could only be bridged by the creator. In other words, a safe harbor was installed for the helmsman to freely navigate about while the oarsmen were left adrift without compass or sail. In times of foul weather, the helmsman strangely possessed a sense of security while the oarsmen relied on their collective wits.

While Dr. William T. Clark brought much-needed reformation to the Home, it was not an experiment in democracy. The Home was a rule-laded institution. Its role was to function like a well-oiled machine, not to embrace. To provide the lubricant, minions were handpicked to report each and every movement of the parts. It was a command-and-control environment.

Frank was one of the chosen. He received his marching orders and was determined not to miss a step. Each day, he would make his daily pilgrimage to the Doc's office, whether at the Home or at camp. It was paramount for the success of Frank that he provide immediate if not somewhat colored information. This was no easy task. The code forbade any kid from divulging information on another kid if the event was negative. And if the event occurred outside of Frank's vision or hearing, he was at a loss. His pipeline closed off, Frank resorted to concocting a story, complete with headline and byline. Immediately, he would don his fedora, grab his coat, and make a beeline for the Doc's office.

"The Doc and I" meeting would be a two-person summit, with the ever-trusted and faultless Ray Chandler in attendance, making copious notations. Once the "I" had spilled his guts, with an occasional nod from the "Doc," the record was established. The offending kid was found guilty by a two-to-nothing vote, with Ray abstaining. Punishment would follow. A safe harbor was established for the "I." Now, the crew would rely on their wits.

Fields, Barns, and Animals

As a boy, nothing beats a good old farm. We would climb apple trees, zigzag through the corn rows, build forts, chase cows, kick pigs, shoot rats, frazzle chickens, build a tree house, and step in "pasture pies." The Home owned a farm situated on prime fertile land, which provided our daily sustenance and provided us with endless adventure. Other than Lynn, a Cornell-bound Home Kid, the boys had no knowledge of animal husbandry or how things grew. Farming was not in our future, but the farm was in our present.

The farm had an in-charge guy by the name of Luke Bell, a one-eyed farmer of unusual strength and endurance. He and his wife lived in one house, and his son-in-law's family lived in the other. There were other employees who resided off the premises. These hardy farmers plowed, cultivated, sowed, and harvested an assortment of crops during the hot and humid summers and the bitterly cold winters. The farm produced corn, wheat, apples, vegetables, milk, butter, eggs, bacon, ham, and beef. Pat Roberts, a teamster, drove the "slop wagon" pulled by a team of horses by the names of Dan and Tony. The wagon had the awful name because it was loaded with the excess and uneaten food from the various residences and hospital. After loading the slop, Pat would drive the team to the sty for the pigs' delight. His son, Russell, eventually married a Home girl. He was genetically fit to carry the household garbage out.

There was a cow barn, a horse barn, a multistoried chicken coop, a pig sty, a creamery, and outbuildings for the storage of farm equipment and machinery. A silo was attached to the cow barn. There were abundant acres of verdant pasture for the dairy cattle and an acrid-smelling dump for the rats. The fields were bounded by a hardwood forest to the east, Welsh Bush Road to the south, the city of Utica to the west, and the Masonic Home to the north. Within those bounds were the fields, barns, and animals, and always, us.

The cow barn was probably the greatest attraction for the boys. This two-story structure contained the dairy cows and two bad-assed bulls, Curly and Sir John, on the ground level and the hayloft on the upper level. Attached to the north side of the barn was a cement-block silo, which collected the harvested corn stored for cattle feed. After several months, the corn would ferment and the cement tube would smell like a Tennessee-hill country still. You would get drunk just by being in the vicinity.

The upper hayloft was home to countless pigeons, starlings, and other winged creatures that would fly in and out of the open barn doors and nest. I don't know what it is about a boy that constantly brings out the spirit of adventure and invincibility. But those birds were mighty tempting targets whether in flight or just roosting and pooping. To meet the challenge, we brought our Wham-O slingshots and pockets full of marbles. For those of us who couldn't afford a one-dollar Wham-O, we constructed slingshots from heavy-duty coat hangers and slices of old bicycle inner tubes.

On Saturday mornings, after choir rehearsal, we headed for the farm with a slingshot stuffed in our dungarees' back pockets and marbles bulging in the front pockets. We were going to war. It was boy versus bird. You would load a marble into the sling, pull back until your hand or the rubber quivered, and let that aggie fly. *Pow!* That marble would ricochet off the steel girders or hit the ceiling. Birds would take to wing, pooping in midflight. This medieval barrage went on for an hour or two until we exhausted our supply of marbles. The birds went unscathed but were scared poopless. Our kill ratio did not deter us, nor did it impress the birds. We kept coming back.

One day, after exhausting our ammo and sitting on bales of hay in dejection, one of the boys discovered a cache of metal roofing brads in wooden kegs. Their shape was perfect for slingshot use, plus they had a killer quality to them—two pointed ends. If slung correctly, these U-shaped projectiles would pierce the thin skin of a bird or stick into the barn's ceiling. (Next to the Molotov cocktail, brads were probably the second most popular weapon of choice by partisan freedom fighters during World War II.) We loaded up on brads and began to fire at will. Again, the brads would ricochet off the girders and ceiling and land in the hay below. About 1 percent of our shots resulted in a kill, while 99 percent fell aimlessly into the hay. If a bird got "nailed," we simply buried it in the hay. War is hell.

This slingshot warfare went on for several more Saturdays. One Monday after the big blue school bus returned to the Home, the boys were summoned to the Wiley Hall library for a "Doc and I" talk. This time, Frank Hall was more serious than usual, and we sensed it. We would have to intently listen and prepare for an instant defense for whatever misdeed occurred.

Mr. Hall waited until there was silence in the room and gave each and every one of us a steely stare through his wire-rimmed glasses. The scene was somber. Sure as hell, the conversation started with "The Doc and I . . ."

Fritz was going to use his boiler room psychology on us. He began by relating his hunting exploits as a young man shooting squirrels, rabbits, and by golly, a deer. His exploits became more expansive and creative on how he stalked his quarry for miles through the forests of the Adirondack Mountains, only to see that his intended prey was a doe and that good sportsmanship commanded that he let the defenseless creature live another day. We sat in stony silence wondering, *Yea, that's neat but what the hell does all this Daniel Boone stuff have to do with us?* After a few more lessons on proper hunting techniques, Frank Hall declared, "Someone killed a cow and Luke Bell is mad as hell! He thinks one of you kids did it, and the Doc and I tend to agree. Goddammit, who did it?"

Frank Hall spoke too long and was about as serious as a clown at the Shrine Circus. He elevated to a rant. "The poor animal ate some hay and up and died!"

A few chosen words of disbelief and grief were uttered in mock sympathy. "Geez, that's awful. Who would kill a poor cow?"

One of the boys overdid it and nearly blew the cover off the mystery of the slain bovine. "Where we gonna get our milk now?"

Fritz ratcheted up another rant with his face reddening. "Luke Bell is going to get to the bottom of this come hell or high water! He doesn't like his cows dying. Who the hell did this!"

We continued being dumbfounded and, at the same time, played a little cat and mouse with Fritz.

"I haven't been up to the farm in months. Besides, I'm afraid of them," one kid confessed.

"I thought we were not allowed on the farm," another answered.

We twisted the Home's rules of restriction to our advantage with great glee. Fritz was beside himself. Having the responsibility of managing a bunch of boys restricted him not to cuss in our midst. He couldn't contain his frustration with his inability to wring the truth out of us. In desperation he exclaimed, "Goddammit, the poor son of a bitch just collapsed in his neck halter and fell to the floor with blood running out of his mouth and nose! His head was still in the halter. He looked like he was lynched! That's a helluva way to go, boys. Think about it."

I never knew that a cow had seven stomachs until Mr. Hall imparted that knowledge. We were in the library, so it was the right place to deliver a veterinarian's sermon. Seven stomachs in a moo-cow? Wow! She must have had a ton of metal in her guts with all the shots we missed. I guess that mass of rawhide would have keeled over from ptomaine poisoning sooner or later.

That last declaratory outburst of anger and emotion did it. We couldn't contain ourselves. Some of us buried our heads into the arms of the chairs to stifle our mirth. One guy abruptly jumped up and dashed out of library, screaming that he had to go pee in a bad way. We looked at each other like a bank of appellate judges pondering a weighty decision. The verdict was in. The jury declared in a chorus, "City kids, Mr. Hall! It was city kids! We saw them hanging around the barn, even told them to leave if they didn't want to get into trouble. We know it was them. Honest to god!"

Thank God for city kids. Once again they got us off the hook by myth or by crook. The city-kid defense worked every time. Although we didn't play the city-kid card too often, it was a solid defense. Fritz accepted the "verdict," but I believe it stuck in his craw that city kids put the "hit" on poor Betsy. Several days later, it was reported that the poor old cow died from multiple lacerations to her many stomachs and other vital body organs. Too much of a "staple" diet, I guess.

City kids were ubiquitous. They were always available in time of need. Like Al Capp's "Shmoos," they could subdivide and multiply whenever the need arose. Frank Hall didn't like city kids because they couldn't be controlled. The Home's prejudice worked to our advantage and was its Achilles' heel.

We stayed clear of the barn for a while. There were plenty of fields, barns, and animals to go around for another day.

The Tree House and Satellite Forts

R oy and I sneaked into the Tonys' place and stole their cigarettes—Camels, Old Golds, Chesterfields, and the green-target Lucky Strikes. Once the cigarettes were purloined, we fled out of the back of the administration building and went hell-bent for the farm. We headed for the tree house, a two-story structure perched within the heavy branches of an old oak on the edge of the cornfield. My brother Jim was the foreman, and Red his apprentice. It was the meeting place away from Wiley Hall. The boys would listen to their high school football team, Proctor, as well as Colgate University whose fullback was Fred Dunlap, our camp counselor.

The tree house was off-limits to us little kids. It was a hideaway for the older boys to smoke cigarettes and look at girlie magazines. The house was lushly furnished with burlap sacks nailed to the inner walls. It had a rope ladder and wooden slats nailed to the trunk as the means of entry. Security was a must.

Roy headed up the ladder. I stayed on the ground and acted as sentry. Once in the tree house, Roy pulled up the ladder and bolted the door. I was stranded on the ground. I pleaded with Roy to drop the ladder, but to no avail. He had the cigarettes, but I had the matches. A standoff. No ladder, huh. I'll smoke him out. I ran to the farm and stole some diesel fuel. I returned, gathered brush and dried corn stalks and poured the fuel and lit the pile.

Boom! The rush and stalks billowed black smoke. Good, I smoked him out. The smoke became fire (that old adage of where there's smoke, there's fire is true). Holy shit! I didn't smoke Roy out, I barbecued him! It was not the "burning bush." It was the whole damn tree and the two-story house. I couldn't see Roy. I lost him.

Luke Bell, his farmers, and the Utica Fire Department came rushing to the scene of the crime. Damn, Frank Hall was right behind. I feared a "Doc and I" talk in the morning.

Someone yelled, "What in the hell happened!"

In defense for my well-being and Roy's life, I blurted, "City kids!"

Frank Hall retorted, "Those wops."

Tears were streaming down my cheeks. I truly believed that Roy was smoked. The thick black smoke began to clear. The edge of the cornfield became visible. There stood Roy with a blackened face smiling, holding up a pack of cigarettes. I slithered away in the other direction while Frank railed about those wops. I never stole cigarettes again.

Every boy needs a fort. It's a rite of passage. Forts are dens of secrecy. You can fart, read girlie magazines, hide BB guns and talk in code about those who made life miserable. At the Home, forts were constructed strategically as to withstand rock throwing and slingshots. The essential building materials consisted of mud, stone, wood, and bark.

Three satellite forts were constructed on various sites in the cow pasture. These were called satellite forts because the tree was the grand tepee and the forts were mere mud huts in comparison. The first fort was christened as the "bark fort." This fort was located behind the left-center field fence of the ball diamond. The "bark fort" was formally known as the Black Hawk Club. This club held formal meetings (well, not that formal because minutes were not kept), and kids held office. The second fort, the "stone hut," was a spin-off of the "bark hut." Some disgruntled members gathered stones and made a makeshift fort that was dug into a hillside. The landscaping was pasture pies complete with flies. The third fort was the brainchild of Johnny Vee. It was fondly referred to as the "mud hut." Located below the horse barn, this structure eliminated the need to gather or peel bark. There was a heavy deposit of clay in the bed of the creek that flowed next to the property. An idea was hatched whereby the hut would be constructed with clay. Another more genius idea was hatched when we decided to build an escape tunnel. Unfortunately, the clay was too hard in the summer, too oozy in the spring, and impenetrable in the winter.

Forts were the foundation of real estate—location, location, location.

Baseball

The game of baseball is America's national pastime. It was ours as well. Baseball had a long tradition at the Home. Every boy had a three-fingered Rawlings or JC Higgins mitt and a thirty-two-inch Stan Musial model Louisville Slugger. The baseball was community property and digressed through various stages of wear. The initial white-leather ball gave way to grass stains, scars, and water weight from being left out overnight. The stitching would begin to unravel until a flap developed. Finally, the worn and tattered cover would be knocked off. Thank God for electrical tape. Several revolutions of this miracle stuff around the ball and you started anew. The only drawback was the game had to end by nightfall so nobody would be hit between the eyes when at the plate or shagging a fly ball.

The Home had its own team replete with uniforms, stockings, and caps. Spikes were a luxury, so high-top sneakers were usually worn. The wool uniforms with Masonic Home stitched in an arc across the chest were uncomfortable in the Utica humidity. They became bearable when worn at the camp because of the lighter air and less humidity in the Adirondacks.

We played against teams from neighboring communities like Boonville, Lyons Falls, Lowville, and Port Leyden. Players from these teams were adult men who farmed, toiled in the sawmills, or chewed tobacco during the day. If we couldn't find a "visiting" team, we played among ourselves. And when we couldn't find enough players among ourselves, we played three-man "pickle" or one-on-one stickball. No matter the circumstances, baseball had to be played. It was more than tradition. It was our holy grail.

In desperate times, there were leaks in the grail. It seems that someone or a Masonic lodge had donated *autographed* baseballs from the Yankees, Dodgers, and Giants. Immortal names—*DiMaggio, Heinrichs, Berra, Rizzuto, Thompson, Mays, Jansen, Hodges, Snider, Robinson*, et al.—were inscribed on various baseballs. These "diamond" gems were kept in a glass case in the library of Wiley Hall. We would stand in awe in front of that case, just itching to hold those priceless rawhide keepsakes. When our makeover baseballs were simply beyond use and in total disrepair, one of the boys would reach into the case and carry the ball out to the backyard, cradling the ball as if it were glassware from the court of Louis XIV. Deftly, the ball would be tossed underhanded to one another until the unpardonable error was committed. My god, a grass stain had smudged *Yogi's* name! No use trying to clean off the stain. Other immortals would face a similar grassy fate. Someone would yell, "Play ball." All was forgiven and forgotten. The code was in effect.

Utica was surrounded by baseball. Boston had the Red Sox and Braves; New York City boasted of three teams—the Yankees, Giants, and Dodgers; Philadelphia had the Phillies and the Athletics; Pittsburgh had the Pirates; and Cleveland had its

Indians. Chicago, Detroit, Saint Louis, and Washington were too far away to capture our imaginations. We huddled around Philco radios to listen to our favorite teams or "borrowed" Wiley Hall's janitor John Loftus's morning newspaper to catch the box scores from the games played the day before. From the beginning of the spring exhibition season to the autumn Fall Classic, baseball consumed our lives.

Baseball is bound by rules—three strikes, four balls, four bases, nine players, hits, runs, errors, and on and on. However, baseball does not require a specific venue. It can be played on a grassy diamond, a vacant lot, a street with parked cars, and even an indoor gymnasium. Our creative venues included a brick-encased elevator shaft or the side of a three-story building of stone and masonry. The teams consisted of one boy each playing pitcher, infielder, and outfielder. The brick wall served as both catcher and umpire. Our baseball was a tennis ball, and the bat would either be a broom handle or a regular baseball bat.

Rules were agreed upon by opposing sides (two boys), strictly adhered to and seldom changed. That maintained the purity of the game that baseball demands for longevity and appeal. There were two sets of rules: one for the Wiley Hall elevator shaft and the other for the three-story wall of the Knights Templar Building.

A chalk outline of the strike zone was drawn on the brick elevator shaft. Imaginary foul lines were drawn approximately forty-five degrees from home plate and extended to as far as the eye could see. A single-base hit had to be hit past the pitcher. A double was a ball hit beyond the third window of the dining hall, which ran down the left field foul line. A triple was a ball hit beyond the fifth window, and a four-bagger was a ball hit beyond the end of the dining hall. An out consisted of a strikeout, catching the ball on the fly, or a one-hop grounder. A double play was enacted when an imaginary runner was on first or first and second or bases loaded and the ball was hit to the pitcher on one hop or a line drive was caught. A triple play was extremely rare and often left up to the combined imagination of both players after an ensuing argument. When the ball was in play, there was a hell of a lot of imagination going on.

Our primary venue was the elevator shaft located on the south side of Wiley Hall. It had an expansive grassy area to accommodate our game, arguments, and imaginations. We seldom had fans. It was simply competitive action between brothers.

The secondary venue was located on the west wall of the Knights Templar building, a massive Gothic structure built in 1917 as a residence for the boys and girls who streamed into the Home after losing a parent or both to the great flu epidemic of 1918. The building later became a residence solely for the girls and eventually was refurbished as a private grammar school for the kids.

The west wall was windowless and possessed a sandstone apron that wrapped around three sides of the building approximately four feet up from its foundation. The apron was constructed so that a slope protruded downward. This slope served as a launching pad for the tennis ball. A player could ignore the slope and simply throw the ball against the wall in order to create a line drive effect, thus catching his opponent flat-footed.

The Knights Templar (KT, for short) site had its list of rules as well. The purity of the game was always at stake and would be observed by any two playing. This venue lacked the inscribed chalk outline and the broom handle and/or bat. A macadam road ran between the KT building and the east side of the

Wiley Hall dining room. It lacked the expansive grassy area that the primary area was blessed with. However, what did make up for the lack of grass was the two-tiered wall on the other side of the blacktopped road. The defensive player could look like Willie Mays with a prodigious leap against the wall and rob the offensive player of a surefire home run. The rules that were applied to the elevator-shaft field were modified to fit the KT field. Baseball integrity was paramount.

My number 1 nemesis was George. We spent a dozen years together at the Home, starting in the nursery and ending up in Wiley Hall. We were two of the big kids now. Our competition was a natural. George was a Brooklyn Dodger diehard, and I was a New York Yankee fan. Whenever the two clashed in the World Series, the Bronx Bombers would always defeat the Bums from Flatbush. Poor "Woody" was in constant heartache while I basked in my glory for another year. George got his revenge in 1955. I didn't get over the loss until after Christmas.

George was the fourth of five children born of Greek parents. He had three older sisters, Maggie, Mary, Katherine, and a younger sister, Barbara. Maggie did a pretty good job on watching George. It was that sibling responsibility that the eldest was saddled with when children entered the Home. The family was an extremely intelligent group who were always at the top of the class scholastically, and George often endured the long hours of tutoring. George himself was self-disciplined and was always on his best behavior. His good-boy demeanor and image was the yin to my mischievous yang.

When out under from his big sister or self-imposed obligations, George and I headed for the elevator shaft with its attendant rules and imaginary foul lines, base hits, and outs. Just as we would arrive at the bricked shaft, George would experience awful stomach cramps. Without failure, the guy had to do a number 2. No rain delay, just a bathroom interruption. Perhaps it was pregame nerves.

George was never really George. Like all the boys at the Home, a nickname was hung on George that would stick for his duration at the Home and beyond. He was known as Woodchuck. This moniker was hung on him by Bill Clark, the superintendent's son, whose own nickname was Moose. I didn't know if George's front teeth were too large or his head had a groundhog's shape or if he was fond of hibernating. I believe he got the tag from his fondness for corn on the cob. In any event, he was always Woodchuck to us.

Our ball games were close affairs: three to two or two to one, maybe a shutout once every so often, but rarely a blowout. One could do wonders with a tennis ball—a sharp curve, a sweeping slider, or a dancing knuckler. Once, I buried a fastball into Woodchuck's ribs (he had men on base), and he let me know in no uncertain terms that he didn't appreciated being "beaned." He being a year older and ten pounds heavier, I didn't protest, but I wasn't afraid to go head-hunting again with the following apology, "Sorry, Woodchuck."

We spent years, days, and hours playing this Home Kid version of baseball. We would reenact our favorite lineups, Rizzuto, Bauer, Berra, Mantle, and other "Pinstripers": Reese, Robinson, Snyder, Hodges, and other "Bums." It was Ford versus Newcombe, Larsen versus Erskine. Stengel would argue with Alston.

We had imaginations. That elevator shaft was Yankee Stadium; the west wall of the KT Building was Ebbets Field. To us boys, America's favorite pastime deserved no better. Maybe we had no one to take us to the ball park, so we brought the ball park to us.

Summer of 1949

The year was 1949. I began my first year of dishwashing at the camp. My older brothers had been dishwashers, so naturally, I was the heir apparent. I was administered a mild oath, "It's in your blood, Kenny." The future looked even bleaker with my hero, Joe DiMaggio, playing his second to the last season as the Yankee center fielder. Joe was going, but Mickey Mantle would replace the $100,000 "Yankee Clipper." Alas, I knew I wasn't going fifty-six consecutive days without breaking a dish, and I was a far cry from being the "Mick." The summer of '49 didn't look too promising for me.

Harry Truman was our President. Gas was twenty-six cents a gallon. First-class postage was a mere three cents. The NYSE was at two hundred, and the minimum wage was forty cents/hour. In the sports world, Joe Louis retired, Sam Snead won the Masters, the New York Giants would sign their first African American, Monte Irvin and Canada routed Denmark in ice hockey, 47 to 0. (The Danes borrowed wooden shoes from Holland.) In the entertainment business, Laurence Olivier and Jane Wyman won Academy Awards, and the songs were dominated by animals—"Mule Train," "Rudolph the

Red-Nosed Reindeer," and "The Pussy Cat Song." In the field of technology, the big bang theory was coined; Albert II, a rhesus monkey, was launched into space; Cadillac was car of the year; and the first Polaroid camera was sold.

Nineteen forty-nine was also the year that Fred and Marilyn Dunlap were appointed as camp counselors. A new era of creativity, teamwork, and self-worth was introduced. The old discipline of command and control took a two-month hiatus. It was the "era of enlightenment."

The camp activities reminded me of the ancient Greek-Roman expressions of art, athletics, and ethics. The games of 1949 began. They made Sunday pine-needle sweeping and afternoon chapel services bearable. The mission statement was "Tomorrow would be another great day."

Competition was keen, tearful, and sometimes downright silly. Sellars and Paul defied *Good Housekeeping* etiquette when, performing a skit, they padded themselves with Dixie cups. (Sellars had one name. His first name was Sellars, as was his last name. If he had a middle name, it would have been the same moniker.) The lake smoother was fair game for any new Home Kid. Future reputations were established with scavenger hunts. I had to forever run to Woodgate to solicit Mrs. Esping's autograph while Tommy forever sat in a boat, fishing for a twelve-inch anything.

I look back in amazement how no one cheated by switching or stealing the opponent's clues during treasure hunts. I guess these were the ethics that Fred and Marilyn instilled into us. Big kids kept pace with the little kids because that was the fair thing to do.

Baseball was not a game unless Marv Allen was umpiring and Henry Kick cheering. Between Marv's vision and Henry's hearing, together with a waffle-iron infield, the game was *Picassoesque.* We were barnstormers traveling to piney Adirondack hideaways like Boonville, Lowville, and Lyons Falls on the back of a three-ton Chevy stake truck.

Ring toss, volleyball, and softball were the opportunities for the boys to display acts of teenage machismo. The goals were to break fingernails, harshly spike the ball, or hit a liner right at her. These goals were realized until Fred showed what tossing, spiking, and hitting a liner was really like when we boys were the targets.

It goes without saying that the summer of 1949 made history with the infamous prison break. The planning for this drama was meticulous and compelling. One early evening, our recreation was interrupted when the superintendent, Dr. Clark, solemnly announced to an assembled group of unsuspecting and innocent juveniles that a prison break had occurred not too far from the camp and three dangerous prisoners were headed our way.

The capture plan was to split up into three squads and head in different directions in order to track and apprehend these heinous criminals. I was assigned to the squad that was to conduct a foray to the dump. With great trepidation, we slithered our way along the lonely road with overhead pines casting images of thirty-foot ghosts.

Two of my comrades-in-arms were Larry and Butchy. Not to be deterred by the sandy road, Larry donned a pair of track spikes. With his cowlicks and an MH brown-and-yellow striped T-shirt, he resembled a cheetah wearing horn-rimmed glasses. Once, as I turned around to check the rear guard, I witnessed an ever-expanding wetness at the confluence of Butchy's trousers' legs. I was fearless for I was clutching my Mini-Trapper pocketknife.

After two hours of trudging, fruitless searches, and bravado threats of retribution upon the escapees, a sudden siren wail erupted through the woods. That was the prearranged signal to return to camp *posthaste*. Afterward, all hell broke loose when Minnie Kinderwater, the nursery matron, complained that she was not made aware of the "break." It was explained to her that the posse formation was on a need-to-know basis. (I believe that she took her angst to the grave.)

We were directed to the recreation hall and given instructions to burst through the doors with pinecones, rocks, and clubs. Again, courage deserted us. We looked like prairie dogs bobbing our heads up and down in order to get a better look-see at the villainous trio. Finally, someone mustered the courage to storm the rec. I held my position in the rear so that I could chronicle the acts of bravery for future generations of Home Kids. My notes described the heroic capture of Rudy "the Predator" Valenzi, Jake "the Snake" Eisenbarth, and Earl "the Quack" Duck—all high-risk escapees. They were caught in the act of devouring ice-chilled watermelon!

As planned, the summer of '49 became a promise. It ended all too soon, though. The Yankees won the Fall Classic. Winter came and went with its usual upstate fury. Spring finally launched with its musty tardiness. I reached double digits in age and was a seasoned dishwasher.

Fred and Marilyn Dunlap were the first authority figures who instilled a positive influence in my life as well as my brother and sister Home Kids. They were a powerful and loving act in the summer of 1949.

The Trout Stream

The most idyllic spot in the entire Masonic Home kingdom was the trout stream. This ribbon of cold, clear water was bracketed by the Long Lake Outlet, a stream that stretched from the southern tip of Long Lake to the confluence of Cummings Creek at Hawkinsville, New York. This outlet coursed through pine forests and fern meadows, with myrtle and eugenia bushes shading its banks. It carved its way through the Adirondack geology that was uplifted, fractured, and eroded for more than a billion years.

Upon exiting Long Lake at Camp Nazareth, the outlet took a southwesterly flow for twenty miles. It flowed between Deer's and Isley's ponds and continued its course for another two miles until it converged with Round Lake's warmer water outlet and thence another seventeen miles to its terminus at Cummings Creek. Never once did this watery arterial merge with any lake or pond. It was fed by several natural springs during its course from Long Lake to the Round Lake outlet. Its waters were clear, pure, and ever so cold.

Between the ponds and the Round Lake outlet flowed the trout stream, a mile of nature's most pristine waters. Its landmarks were few—a pump house that quietly siphoned its sweet water, a wooden bridge of dubious character, the radical bend at the end of Hog's Back Ridge, three beaver dams, and two sandbars. Nature had been kind to this quiet and meandering stream. No outside poachers found its banks. City kids were too far away. There were no holy wars between the Catholic kids at Camp Nazareth and the orphan kids at the Masonic Home. It was ours. And it was Doc Clark's.

I was introduced to the trout stream by my brother Jim. Nursery kids were forbidden to be on their own without a matron or, with permission from the matron, an older, responsible kid. My brother, who was six years older than me, passed the older qualification and lied about being responsible. He took me beyond all camp buildings and civilization, into the forest and toward the depression created by the uplifted Hog's Back Ridge, where the sacred waters flowed.

The bushes were taller than my five-year-old body and were quite formidable to walk through. Jim hoisted me up on his shoulders, and we walked the fifty yards to the stream. What an amazing day! I caught my first brook trout—a dazzling beauty with a green dorsal, orange underbelly, and yellowish dots. It would be a long time before I would have a similar day. Upon our return, my brother told the matron that he took me on a hike to the lean-to cabin across the lake.

As the years passed, I no longer had to take "a hike to the lean-to cabin across the lake." I was older and somehow passed the responsibility test. The only barrier in my way was the inability to be in two places at once. (I longed for an identical twin brother that the Home would have no knowledge of, someone like a city kid who knew Home Kid ways.) The activities, while challenging and fun, were regimentally scheduled. First bugle call at 0700, breakfast at 0730, wash dishes, change clothes, and activities from 0900 to 1100 hours. Swimming from 1100 to 1200, lunch, wash dishes, change clothes, activities from 1400 to 1600 hours, more swimming, dinner, wash dishes, change clothes, more activities from 1800 to 1900, recreation hall until 1930, night lunch, and finally, taps at 2000 hours. Next day, same routine. I liked what we did, but I also liked fishing. My intermittent mantra was "Please rain." Some days were declared as "free days." The girls headed for the swimming dock to perfect their tans, some boys loafed, listened to the radio, while some of us hard core headed for the holy grail of Adirondack waters.

Rain brought a free day, and it brought the worms. Before heading for the stream, a quick dash down to Isley's farm to dig for worms was in order. With a tin can chock-full of earthworms, we headed for paradise. Once up the blacktop road, we turned left at the three "doughnuts." The doughnuts were concrete culverts about six feet in length and the same in diameter that were part of the landscape for want of another use. A half-mile hike along the spine of the Hog's Back and we would slip down through the myrtle bushes and disappear.

Each of us would stake out our favorite hole, careful not to trespass into the other guy's spot, and cast away with a gob of worm, split shot sinker, and a number 8 snell hook on the end of the line. We would camouflage ourselves near or under a bush, in ice-cold water up to our waist and beyond, occasionally ducking under the water to rid ourselves of the pesky black flies that swarmed about our heads. Occasionally, a brook trout would break water to munch those same black flies. It was not a symbiotic relationship. It was more like a paper-scissors-rock relationship. Fly gets man; man gets trout, and trout gets fly. That was one of Izaak Walton's laws.

The other pest was Honey, a "Heinz fifty-seven variety" dog of various breeds. The dog belonged to Marv Allen, the camp's caretaker, wheeze-whistler, and part-time baseball umpire. Honey was a loner, yet craved love and slept under the boys' cottage. When June rolled around, the dog experienced heightened anxiety waiting for the kids to show up to the camp for two months. For the remaining ten months, the dog must have gone into deep depression for lack of playmates. Her only entertainment was listening to Marv's wheeze-whistle. Whoever was farthest from the main camp, Honey was the constant companion. When we visited the trout stream, Honey would dash through the bushes and be with the fisherman who was farthest away, even if it meant another twenty yards. Unfortunately, during the deer hunting season, a hunter mistook Honey for a whitetail buck. That son of a bitch of a hunter would have mistaken one of us kids as the abominable snowman.

Suddenly, from around the bend, you could hear, "Got one!" Then, in dejection, "Shit, it's a chub." As the day wore on, there were excited claims of victory over the trout. The dialogue of "Shit/Got one!" went on throughout the day. Once in a while, this dichotomous dialogue would be punctuated with a "Goddammit!" This usually was the alarm that one of us fell off a beaver dam or walked off a sand ledge into deep water. As long as you held on to your rod and kept the worms relatively dry, you were still in paradise on earth and not in some icy, watery realm.

I learned that trout watch the weather better than people. They seek the shade of the underbrush on hot days. They like a quick swim in the rain. Shadows and noise are bothersome like an elderly lady in the public library. If the food doesn't look good, they won't eat it. If a big guy comes into the neighborhood, the little guys scurry for home. I realized early on that the brook trout is the "phantom of the eddy."

Whenever the sun drew high in the sky, the bite was off. Fishing came to a standstill. The trout were in a siesta mode, and the chub was the only creature knocking on your hook. The black flies never slept. You still made your vertical drop into the icy waters and held your breath long enough for the critters to get bored and fly off in formation to the next paper-scissors-rock victim.

This lull in the fishing was particularly challenging for Bernie. Bernie was the younger brother to Tom and was the recipient of the family gene pool for humor. He was the Home's jokester. He administered and received humor in equal amounts. He had a distinct ability to imitate any noise created on the face of the earth. It could be a bus applying its brakes, the trill of a bird, a blast of air, a trout fart, an old man blowing his nose, a bullet fired from a pistol, or wax being pulled from an ear. It didn't matter. If an event made a noise regardless of its decibel level, Bernie could reinvent the identical noise—tone, timbre, pitch, and intensity. During our excursions to the trout stream and when fishing came to a lull, Bernie would announce to the entire world the sign-off code to the mythical radio station, BFG, "Ba-fon-goool" with the same intonation as the National Broadcasting Company's chimes. The rest of us would erupt in laughter, knowing that Bernie had bellowed an Italian expletive.

When we returned to the camp, the boys loafing on their bunks or listening to the radio would say, "Geez, we heard you guys way over in the trout stream. Catch any?"

The stream also belonged to Doc Clark, an avid angler. While we toiled with our endless activities, Doc Clark would steal away, rain or shine, and fish those same waters that we claimed as our youthful right.

We had done a pretty good number on several of the accessible holes. Doc Clark would not take the risk and wedge into some of our fishing spots. He realized that a troop of four to five boys would claim more trout than he by himself. Without telling a soul, he purchased (by someone's count) sixty beautiful brook trout and planted them in his accessible hole. We knew it was his hole because he left his cigarette filters on the sandbar.

Well, Mother Nature cooperated and created a rainy day. No regimented routines. A free day was proclaimed, and the troop headed for the trout stream. It was a day to beat all days forever and ever. We caught fifty-six trout, all legal size, and the bag limit set by the state of New York did not apply to our private, heavenly trout stream. We brought every one of those speckled beauties home to show off to anyone and everyone. The collective inquiry was "Geez, you guys caught those in the trout stream?" The collective response was "Yep."

Of course, Frank Hall saw our bounty, and as usual, he headed straight for the Doc's summer cottage perched on a hill overlooking Round Lake and gave him the "good news." I wish that I was a fly of the knotty pine wall to hear firsthand the "Doc and I" conversation. "The boys caught fifty-six trout, Doc. Wow, that's something for a bunch of kids."

"Frank, you say fifty-six trout! Yeah, that *is* something for a bunch of kids." *The little bastards*, he must have thought. I would like to believe that when the Doc came to his senses, he believed that it was our trout stream as well. As far as we were concerned, he still owed us four more trout.

I didn't know much about life or death, but I was willing to spend the rest of my days on the trout stream.

Five o'clock in the Morning

ound Lake is situated in the midst of 1,600 acres of
pine, spruce, balsa, birch, and a host of other hardwood
trees. Within three miles of its treelined banks, Round Lake has
an assortment of sister ponds. To the north were Deer's and
Isley's ponds. To the south was Mud Pond. As adventuresome
kids, we normally avoided these outlying ponds because of
their muddiness, shallowness, and lack of fish. Mud Pond was
filled with leeches, and Deer Pond was the "land of the quaking
earth." Round Lake was fed by an underground spring, with a
water lily-covered outlet. Its pristine waters made it the crown
jewel of the Masonic Home Camp. This 1,600-acre Adirondack
oasis was the source of all water activities.

Each summer, the boys and girls spent two glorious months
swimming, hiking, doing athletics, sunbathing, and the
Olympus of all events—fishing. This was the place to cast that
open-face South Bend reel with black threaded line attached to
a Pflueger steel rod. Tie on that number 6 Eagle Claw hook, bait
it with a worm, night crawler, or the freshwater cyprinid known
as the minnow. Fishing was not an avocation or something to do
while passing time. It was the essence of my being while at the

camp. I would pray for rainy days. When it rained, all scheduled activities were cancelled and you would idle your time in the rec hall or lie in your bunk. Rain and fishing were like Damon and Pythias, friends forever devoted to one another and to me.

Fishing was in my blood. My older brothers were avid fishermen since their days living on the California coast. Bob, the second oldest, was always on the lake, fishing in solitary fashion. I begged and cajoled him to take me with him, but to no avail. He always had a reason for leaving me on the banks. He would explain that the water was too deep for me, that fish only prefer one baited hook in the water or the sun was low on the horizon. I took his word as gospel. I attempted to get on his good side and do him a favor and fetch bait. I asked him what bait he was using, and like the wise sixteen-year-old angler he was, he said he preferred flies. Off I ran to the barn, balanced precariously on two stacked chairs, and began to pick houseflies from the sticky flypaper coiled down from the ceiling. I believed my brother was giving me future advice that fishing is a sport for the solitary.

My uncles were likewise avid fishermen in the province of Ontario, Canada. With an "eh" they would go "oot and aboot" into the Canadian wildness fishing for the great northern pike, grayling, muskie, and trout. My uncle Norman took up permanent residence with the Cree natives of northern Ontario. Yes, fishing was a genetic passion.

With my brothers cutting me loose (using baseball parlance) I was fortunate and eternally grateful to have my option picked up by Tom, a Home Kid two years older than me. Tom too came from a lineage of devoted fishermen. His uncles, especially Ormond, were renowned for their angling prowess throughout the Mohawk Valley and Adirondack Mountains. Tom was a quick learner and was eager to teach. I was ready and willing. Izaak Walton couldn't have made a better fishing duo.

Being two years older, Tom was wise beyond his years. He was wily, yet gentlemanly, in his approach to life at the Home. He assumed a great burden when he entered the Home and his father told him that he was now the surrogate father to his three younger siblings—Natalie, Bernie, and Patty. Children were separated by age and gender. Thus, Tom had to navigate through two rule-laden dormitories in order to assume his fatherly role. Being a twelve-year-old father in a parentless world was an awesome responsibility.

Tom was athletic, an outdoors kid, an excellent student, and an artist who had an unequaled eye for the girls. His charming manner and good looks often conflicted with others' perceptions of his Italian roots. He was a kid from east Utica, formerly a city kid and very proud of his Italian heritage. Tom was in a new environment with multiple ethnicities yet dominated by the Anglo-Saxon/Protestant rules of obedience. The head of the Tonys, the grounds-maintenance workers, was his paternal grandfather. Some of the housepainters were his uncles. Tom lived in two worlds. He was forced to tiptoe through both.

Nineteen fifty-five would be Tom's last summer at the camp, and he wanted to make the most of it. The following year, he was to graduate from high school. Graduation was more than completing high school. It was a time of torn feelings, a time of personal satisfaction, and yet, a time of personal fear. This was the time that you were leaving the Home, leaving your brothers and sisters, leaving the memories that were so indelible. There was no turning back. There was one unhappy way in and one unknown way out. Your own your now, kid. This would be a summer to remember.

Tom and I made a pact that we would arise at 5:00 am each every morning, come rain or shine, and fish for bass on Round Lake. That was two hours of uninterrupted, nonstop fishing: lingering in our favorite holes, trolling across the lake twice, or looking for new underwater fish nests along the banks. It was a time for competition between two boys, not only for fishing but for one another's attention and approval. Our lake-level conversations were about baseball, girls, and the ineptitude of the administration of the Home. Like most teenagers, we were judgmental of others and especially critical of the boys' matron. Tom and I were in agreement on most things except the Yankees and Red Sox.

Getting up every morning at 5:00 am was a commitment. No alarm clocks and no one to give you a nudge. Luckily, Tom had a built-in clock that wakened him precisely at five in the morning. He would whisper across the aisle toward my bunk, "Kenny, it's time to get up. Let's go."

After the first couple of early-morning whispers couched within Tom's frowns, I had no problem with the early risings. Tom convinced me that fish love cold mornings and that if we were not on the lake before the sun rose, then forget about the fish. I found the chilly Adirondack mornings invigorating for both me and the fish.

Our fishing gear was readied the night before. Like firemen, we slept half-dressed. When Tom's inner alarm went off, we rose, put on our sneakers, grabbed our gear, and ambled down to the boat dock. The walk down to the lakeside was rather eerie. The stars were still out, and so were the bats. The tall pines cast ghostly shadows across our paths. There were always stories handed down from the older boys that wildcats and bears would stalk boys on the way to the dock. We walked with one hand gripping our rods, the other toting the tackle box, with our heads bobbing and weaving, watching for flying bats and wild animals lying in wait.

Bait was the catalyst for successful fishing. Our bait primarily consisted of earthworms or minnows. The worms were dug up from Isley's farm about a mile from the main camp. It was the only place with earthy soil within walking distance. The soil in the Adirondacks is sandy and granulated granite from the millennia of the Earth's geologic upheavals. It amazed me how that plot of soil yielded so many worms over the years. Old man George Isley must have dumped his table scraps and roadkill back of his barn.

Minnows, on the other hand, took more energy and care to trap and preserve. Somehow, Tom was able to cajole me into applying for and being granted that task. He flattered me by saying, "Kenny, you're a runner, and the spring is about two and half miles roundtrip. I'll scout the lake for tomorrow's fish locations."

Running to the spring was accomplished *after* my lunch dishwashing chores and *before* compulsory afternoon activities. Wash dishes for seventy-five people, change into my dungarees, grab the minnow trap, run like hell to the spring, bait and set the trap, and run back. This assignment was repeated after dinner with the additional responsibility of carrying the minnows back in a three-gallon bucket without loss of minnow or water.

Tom's assignment was trolling with a flatfish lure while someone else manned the oars. Of course, at the time, I was running, Tom was trolling. That assignment was never altered. Tom was the fish locator, and I was the minnow locator. Tom said it was an equal distribution of responsibility. I thought it was an unequal distribution of labor.

Once at the dock, it became a question of which boat to take. They appeared to have been manufactured in a sieve factory for levee construction. The boats were wooden hulled and weighed about four hundred pounds. These sixteen-foot tubs were equipped with oarlocks with a guarantee of at least one being inoperable. The seats across the beam were rock-hard wood. A one-gallon, concrete-filled paint can was the anchor. No matter how much preparation was done the night before, you could be assured that the following morning water would be sloshing up to the gunwales. Naturally, and for survival's sake, we took the boat with the least amount of water.

We stowed our gear, and with a shove, we were off. Once again, the division of labor was at issue. I rowed and Tom trolled. The explanation given by Tom was that rowing would strengthen my stamina for running, and trolling would perfect his ability to locate the fish. Huffing and puffing, I consented. Any labor expended for fishing was worth the effort.

Adirondack mornings provide the essence of nature. Easterly sunrises warmed the lake that would create misty white plumes just above lake surfaces. Hidden within the mist, loon pairs would warble their haunting calls then suddenly disappear below the surface for an early-morning breakfast. The shimmering waters would reflect the trio of birches standing like sentinels on the banks of the lake. Open-air stone summerhouses guarded the 120-degree arcs of Round Lake. The outlet presented its daily display of white and yellow water lilies. At the other end, gray smoke would curl from the chimney at the Dell'armi house. The Dell'armi family was the original owners of the camp property. The family sold the property to the New York State Grand Lodge of Masons in 1923 as a summer camp for Home residents. As part of the sale, the Dell'armis retained their family home as well as a cemetery tucked in the forest behind Pine Point.

There was a need for my rowing. Other than trolling, my partner-brother took the Adirondack mornings to mind and heart. Tom was an artist.

For two hours, we whiled the time away by catching an assortment of perch, bullhead, shiners, sunfish, rock bass, and occasionally, the beast of fish—smallmouth black bass. Everything was returned to the lake with the exception of a legal-sized black bass. This scaly creature was the trophy, your bragging rights, your bring-it-back for all to see and hopefully envy. You hit the double jackpot if Dr. Clark, the Home's superintendent and himself an avid fisherman, took recognition of your prize.

Fishing and sleeping ceased when Georgie V. blew reveille at 7:00 am. The second bugle blast would occur precisely fifteen minutes later. That was the signal to grab the oars and head back to the dock. Not too fast, Tom had to troll. Georgie was punctual to a fault. He took his bugler duties with great pride and timeliness, making sure that each note was not a clunker despite the boys pulling his pants down in the midst of his reenactments of World War I clarion calls. Each day started with a staccato blast and ended up with the doleful taps.

One crisp July morning, with both rods in the water, the two of us began our daily recap of last night's baseball scores. Tom would fire the first salvo: "I heard where you guys beat the Senators, again. Is that all the Yankees play?"

I fired back, "Geez, the Red Sox beat that minor league team, the Saint Louis Browns. Does Yawkey pay the Browns to play the Bosox?"

The banter continued. You had to maintain a low decibel level while on the lake. There is some weird law of physics that says a voice carries like a sonic boom when vocalized on water. It was a corker when out of the middle of the lake, one of the boys would bellow a meaningful, staccato rendition of "shit!" Invariably, it brought out a stern lecture from the "Doc and I."

That morning, I looked beyond Tom and fixed on that column of stone masonry that stood by the swimming beach. I had viewed that column for eleven years and never really paid attention to it. In the usual hushed tones, I asked Tom, "What is that thing over there by the beach? I've seen it for years and never understood what the hell it is."

Tom, with just a hint of historical trivia about his lips, answered, "That's my grandfather's dick."

"Your grandfather's what?" I was dumbfounded.

"His dick, his pecker. You know what a pecker looks like, don't you, Kenny? Christ, look at it," Tom insisted.

While studying this stone column, Tom gave me the history of the "dick." During the building phase of the camp, the boys and the Tonys were instrumental in the construction of the buildings. As an artistic statement, Tom's grandfather, a reader of ancient mythology, applied a Medusian stare and erected (not to make a pun) a symbolic, larger-than-life, fully circumcised stone phallus. I began to appreciate Tom's love of the arts.

In August, the Adirondack mornings become chillier with the mist creating a blanket of thick fog. Visibility is cut to ten feet. I had to be extra precautious and not row into the swimming dock or White Bridge. Tom would be quick to rejoin that his trolling went for naught. We maintained a vigilant watch on those mornings.

One August morning, we made our early morning trek down to the boat dock. The overnight fog had deposited an unusual amount of water into the tubs. Bailing out water from these water-soaked wagons was a waste of precious fishing time. This particular August morning was the dawn of Dr. Clark's sixty-something birthday. No way was he going fishing on his birthday. Besides, Mrs. Clark would have a birthday present for her husband while in bed. This time, Tom's caution was overridden by my brass.

"Why not take the Doc's boat?" It was clean, dry as a bone, and the oarlocks didn't squeak. "It would be pure stealth sneaking up on the bass this foggy morning."

I rowed and Tom trolled to our usual first hole off Star Point. The minnows were fresh. They became agitated when they hit the cold water and headed for cover, the same cover where smallmouth black bass lurk. Each of us sensed a lake record in a matter of minutes.

However, in a matter of minutes, we heard the familiar squeak of the oarlocks. Unlike a summer storm, we could hear the sound before the image appeared.

"Who the hell is that?" I queried in hushed tones.

Tom, being guarded, replied, "How do I know, suppose it's Doc Clark!"

Fishing became a secondary thought. Self-preservation became preeminent in our minds. We contemplated weighing the paint can of concrete and rowing like hell to the far-reaches of the outlet, well hidden by the thick fog.

This time, Tom prevailed. My brass turned into soft tin.

"He's going to know it's us, Kenny. We're out here every morning. Why run? There's no city kids up here. Let's just sit here and wait. Maybe he'll row right by us and not spot us through the fog," Tom cautioned.

We froze. Our minnows threw in the towel. The concrete anchor was still hugging the bottom of the lake. The end was in sight.

The squeaks got louder. You could hear the water slapping against the water wagon. A faint image of a sole fisherman became clearer. What did the captain say about don't do anything until you see the whites of their eyes?

In unison, "Good morning, Dr. Clark. Happy birthday!"

Without hesitation, "Would you like your boat? Being your birthday and all, we thought you'd sleep in this morning."

The response caught us off guard and was most reassuring. "Thanks, boys. You go ahead and use my boat. Catch anything?"

The quid pro quo was "You're welcome," and we rowed like hell for the outlet.

Two weeks later, we ran out of 5:00 am adventure and fun. I learned how to row. I could recognize a stone "dick." I learned to say "Happy birthday" in the fog. I sought my soul, but my soul I could not see. I sought my peace, but my peace eluded me. I sought my brother and found all three.

February 15, 1958

Saturday, February 15, 1958—nothing of world or national importance occurred on that snowy Saturday. Three days prior, I got one of those "the Doc and I" messages from Frank Hall. This time I was dumbfounded. I stayed out of trouble for a year, received Bs and As in school, won third place in the New York State Cross Country championship, and became master councilor of the local DeMolay Chapter. I was good without having to kiss ass. Colleges were offering me scholarships, all of which impressed me.

I had graduated in January, skipped PG (postgraduate studies), obtained a job working for the Utica Road Department. I admit, the only ass-kissing was to remain at the Home for room and board. What the hell? Others had done it before me. Some went off to the service and returned to the Home to live and eat for free. Alas, that path was closed to me years earlier. No amount of ass-kissing would restore my good-boy status.

On Wednesday, Frank Hall and I walked that "last mile" to the Doc's office. We trudged through the snow from Wiley Hall to that gothic administration building, which gave the appearance that Count Dracula resided in its lower bowels only to flap his wings to the upper rafters, four stories higher. It was not a friendly place. The Tonys ruled the lower world with their cousins, the painters, nearby. The second floor was lorded over by the Doc and his able administrators. The third and fourth floor were vacant with the exception of a Home Kid returned.

The Doc's office was as usual. His back to the windows in order for you to stare into the low winter sun. Lights were dimmed in this cavernous office laden with lavish and cumbersome wood. It gave the appearance of authority. The odds were not in favor of the one seated in front of the Doc, who made sure that his desk lamp was lowered to an angle to evoke fear and being uncomfortable.

Frank and I sat immediately and quietly while the Doc studied a piece of paper. I thought that that sole piece of paper contained my entire Masonic Home existence. After a fashion he moved my "existence" toward my direction. My heart was pounding, my eyes a bit teary, and my body trembled ever so slightly. My "existence" was a check in the amount of $125. At first I thought it was an advance for my room and board until the Doc set me into reality.

"This, Kenny, is your one way ticket to California. I called your father's lodge and told them that you were leaving the Home. Your father's lodge donated $250." With that the Doc purchased a one-way ticket to Los Angeles, and I received the balance. I felt like a prisoner being set free.

Thereafter, Frank Hall escorted me to the memorial building (another gothic remnant) and told me to pick out a trunk. Christ! Johnny and I had handpicked the best, and I was left with empty secondhands.

Thursday and Friday were spent packing (not much) and mooching a ride to Proctor High School to say my good-byes. The last Home Kid I bade good-bye was ironically the first—Johnny, that swarthy kid, now a young man.

Saturday, February 16, 1958, I boarded Mohawk Airlines and abruptly hopscotched my way to Los Angeles, California, after 4,963 days living among my newly found but never ending brothers and sisters.

Appendix

WHY WE COME BACK

When I was asked to be your spokesman on this occasion, our biennial reunion of Masonic Home Kids, I asked myself, why me? when I know there are others among us who can do a more creditable job than I. I cannot tell you anything more about this Home and our experience here than you already know. After long thought, I decided to talk about why we come back, time and again, to the Masonic Home, truly our home for many years. What is it that draws us like a large, powerful magnet back to this place? Have we ever really left it?

Many years have passed since we entered and left the Home through those large swinging gates on Bleecker Street but we both know and have known all these years that it is the strong yet tender force of love that you and I have for each other and for the love Masons shared with all of us. Tragic circumstances brought us together but it was the love that we as children of God experienced—the love our parents had for us; our fathers, upright men and Masons, for making it possible to have this shelter, this home, for us to come to in our hour of dire need; and our mothers for having the love and courage to bear the separation from their children so that their children could receive the best of care, guidance and love that one human could give to another.

Who can ever forget the wounds we children suffered, the loss of our loved ones, the fear, the loneliness, the desolation, standing naked in a hostile world in which we found ourselves. That was how you and I met, then learned to love and have affection for each other as brother, sister and friend. I remember only too well those nights when all of my hidden emotions would overwhelm me and how I would bury my head in my

pillow to stifle my sobs so that you wouldn't hear me or see the tears
I shed and know the loneliness and fear I felt. But you heard me and
knew what I was passing through. I couldn't fool you. You felt love and
compassion for me as you tried to comfort me in my darkest hours. I felt
your presence, your hand on my shoulder and felt the tears you shed for me.
You knew, for hadn't you been here before me? I couldn't fathom it then
but I found out later that it was love you gave and shared with me. And
I, too, learned from you, to give and share my love with you, my
brother and sister. How can I ever forget you?

After all these years we can clearly see how Masonry has played a
great part in our lives. Its basic tenets of Friendship, Morality,
Brotherly Love, Relief and Truth are demonstrated in this Masonic Home,
a living and dynamic memorial to mankind of the work Masons do, not only
here but throughout the world, the work of the Great Architect Of The
Universe in the betterment and uplifting of mankind. Who can deny that
we children have seen, felt and touched the heart of Masonry and lived
for a brief hour in its bosom? We have been fortunate, indeed!

Early on, we learned about Friendship and Loyalty, that I could
turn to you for guidance and support in my time of need and know that I
was not alone. We learned about Morality, to walk uprightly with
honesty and integrity, decency, modesty and humility, and take pride in
ourselves. We became united in Brotherly Love and Affection, learning
respect and responsibility, fostering a heartfelt benevolence for another
human being, trying to help lift him off his cross of pain and suffering.

These principles, through our Masonic Home experience, have become a part of us, helping us through the moving currents of Life and revealing to us who we are and why we are here. We can see the practice of Masonic Relief and Truth which we have had the privilege and good fortune to experience first-hand. This then is really what Life is all about, that we are of the same Creator and must help and love each other as we learned at the Masonic Home. If we have not learned from our own pain and suffering to understand that of others, then our own has been wasted on us.

When we left the Home, a chapter in our lives was over, but what we shared will never be over. Our presence here today is visible proof of this. I am sure that when the time arrives to depart this life, you and I will meet again in another time and another place. The Masonic Home was the focal point for our present encounter in this lifetime. Even though our arrival at this time and place was soul-shaking, I am grateful that it was here, the Masonic Home, where you and I met as strangers, learned to love one another and know that we are brothers and sisters, helping each other, in true Masonic spirit, on our Life's eternal journey. We are indeed fortunate to have been reared in our Masonic Home under the guidance and love of Masons, people who practice what they believe in--the Brotherhood of Man under the Fatherhood of God.

I could go on talking for hours about details of our life in the Home which I know you carry in your heart. The bittersweet memories we have of those years, the lessons we learned, the good and not-so-good experiences which make up the fabric of our lives have helped us build a solid foundation on which to live a life capable of withstanding the onslaughts we face during our lifetimes--the war years, the loss of our loved ones at home and those who served in our struggle to stay alive and remain free, the economic and personal ups and downs we face in our lives daily. Yes, they taught us well in our formative years.

As each year passes, we lose our brothers and sisters little by little which saddens us. We find that all we can ever really take with us are those intangibles, the memories and love we have shared in our times together during our climb upwards on the ladder of Life. So we hold dear our early years together.

I would like to share with you a recent experience. It was Memorial Day, 1987. I was visiting the grave of my beloved wife, Eleanor, a World War II Navy nurse, whom I had lost in 1980 due to cancer. She is buried in Calverton National Cemetery along with thousands of other veterans. In order to locate her grave (since there are no visible markers, but rather bronze plaques lying flat on the ground on the grave), I would count so many bronze plaques to the right of a certain tree and then nine graves up to hers. As I started my count from the tree, I stumbled and accidentally stepped on the third bronze plaque, caught myself, straightened up to continue my search. Something impelled me to look down before leaving. I couldn't believe it! I had stumbled onto the grave of one of my closest chums from the Home. He had died and was buried about a month to the day after my wife's demise. Here his remains had been for seven years, not more than thirty feet away from her grave— and I never knew it until then. The last time we had seen each other was twenty-five years ago when he visited me and my family at my home. Even in death we touch each other. So you see, have we ever left the Home?

In closing, I would like to say that I am thankful for Life, for

APPENDIX

having the opportunity to be with you and your loved ones once again, to
renew old friendships and share memories which are so precious to each
of us. We are grateful for the privilege granted us by the Board of
Trustees of the Masonic Home in allowing us to come home. We extend our
thanks with love and appreciation to all Masons who made it possible for
us, their children, to have a a home when our need was so great. Masons
are truly in the service of God. I am indebted to the poet and philosopher
who wrote the following:

> "I sought my Soul, but my Soul I could not see;
> I sought my God, but my God eluded me;
> I sought my Brother, and found all Three."

May God bless you, keep you and be with you till we meet again. I
am your brother,

                    Frank.